LOCAL OFFICIALS GUIDE

Making Government Work For Your City's Kids

Getting Through The Intergovernmental Maze of Programs For Children and Families

By Bonnie Armstrong

National League of Cities

CONTENTS

FOREWORD

"It is squarely a municipal job to help weave the community fabric that can strengthen families and neighborhoods."
Donald Fraser, Mayor
Minneapolis, Minnesota
and First Vice-President
National League of Cities

There is a patchwork of services to children and families in our cities and towns. Some services are provided by the federal or state government; some are provided by the county or municipal government; others are provided by the schools; and still others are provided by a private agency or institution. This patchwork can create confusion, questions of jurisdiction, and an attitude of "let someone else do it."

The National League of Cities (NLC) is pleased to present this new guidebook to assist municipal officials work through this intergovernmental maze. *Making Government Work for Your City's Kids* describes various governmental processes that affect children and families and provides examples of how municipal officials can affect those processes.

This book is the latest in a series of products, activities, and publications from NLC's Children and Families in Cities Project. It is carried out under the leadership of John E. Kyle, with the assistance of Serita Kelsey and Tonya Gary. The Project is one part of a broad NLC strategy to help local officials in regard to meeting the needs of children and families in their communities. Other significant parts of the strategy include the "family-friendly communities" focus of the Futures Process being conducted by NLC's Advisory Council, the reports and studies by the Task Forces on Education and on the Future of Youth, and the ongoing work of the Human Development Committee.

We congratulate Bonnie Armstrong on writing this important book and John Kyle on developing the original concept and shepherding the project to completion.

We express our thanks to Carnegie Corporation of New York and to the Lilly Endowment, whose grants are supporting the ongoing work of the Project on Children and Families in Cities, including this new book.

We welcome comments and questions from readers because we are committed to continually improving how we assist municipal officials, local governments, state municipal leagues, and others interested in "making government work for your city's kids."

Donald J. Borut
Executive Director

William R. Barnes
Director,
Center for Research and Program
Development

PREFACE

Writing this book has been an energizing experience that has underscored my faith in the old adage: "Think globally, act locally." It is invigorating to know that, in the midst of a recession and the recurring bad news about how poorly children and families are faring, optimistic and committed public officials in communities all over the country are working hard to improve conditions for their neighbors. I had the good fortune to talk to dozens of them, and each one was happy to help—eager to share insights and pass on lessons learned. My thanks to all of you who completed a questionnaire or answered my calls.

As we worked to define the type of intergovernmental relations information that would be useful to local officials as they try to meet the needs of children and families, John Kyle and I consulted several people who represent different perspectives. Jean McIntosh of the Child Welfare League of America, Kim Chudoba from the League of California Cities, Bonnie Politz of the Annie E. Casey Foundation, Judy Weitz of KIDS COUNT, City Council President Maryann Mahaffey of Detroit, and City Council Member Tom Werth of Rochester, Michigan, all helped. They have our appreciation.

In collecting information, I also received enthusiastic assistance from a variety of organizations around the country. All of the organizations listed as resources in the text were eager to share their expertise in a way that could be useful to local officials. If you decide to contact any of them, I am confident that they will do everything in their power to help you meet the needs of your city's families.

Two people deserve special thanks for helping in the conceptualization and information-gathering phases, and for taking the time to review and comment on an early draft. Sid Gardner and Nancy Amidei gave unselfishly of their time, experience, and creativity and improved the product you see. In addition, Frances Huntley-Cooper, Mayor of Fitchburg, Wisconsin; Elaine Pfalzgraf, Council Member, Cedar Falls, Iowa; and Dr. Michael Pagano, Professor of Political Science, Miami University, Oxford, Ohio, wrote helpful critiques, and several NLC staff members, including Bill Barnes, Serita Kelsey, Janet Quist, Kate Herber, Thom McCloud, and Julio Barreto, made thoughtful suggestions on the first draft. Thanks to all of you.

Katie Nack, city councilwoman and former member of the school board in my hometown of Pasadena, California, made herself available for consultation at each step along the way and also reviewed a draft. I thank her for her help and also for all that she has done for the children of our community.

John Kyle's vision has brought this book to reality. He is a thoughtful and perceptive part of the paradigm shift that is bringing local government back into the forefront of human services. I am particularly grateful for his reminders to stay focused on the topic at hand, when my own passions sometimes caused me to want to take on more issues than could be appropriately handled in one book.

Pat Morrison's illustrations add life to the text, and Clint Page's editing, layout, and production have made the entire document more interesting and readable.

INTRODUCTION

The Children and Families in Cities Project is a continuing effort by the National League of Cities to encourage and enable local elected officials to meet the needs of children and families through direct assistance, research, policy analysis, and networking. One of the Project's goals is the development of effective local leadership that understands

- **how to make intergovernmental systems work,**

- **how to take full advantage of available resources, and**

- **how to have an impact on local, state, and national agendas on behalf of children and families.**

This guidebook is part of that process. Together with the other publications of the project, it provides a framework for effective local action. *Your City's Kids*, published in 1988, outlines how you can begin to raise local awareness about the issues facing children and families and to get your community involved in improving the conditions affecting children and families. *Ways and Means For Children and Families*, published in 1991, is a detailed guide to finding, brokering, and leveraging funding sources for the benefit of your community's children and families.

The purpose of this book is to help you, as a local elected official, become a better intergovernmental advocate for your city's children and families. Intergovernmental advocacy is a dynamic and interactive pursuit in which relationships can be as important as knowledge. Therefore, you may wish to use the information in this book as the basis for workshops, seminars, or networking meetings where local officials, staff members, and other advocates can energize each other, share successes and frustrations, and develop strategies for new local solutions.

In preparing this document, the counsel and experience of the members of selected NLC committees were sought. A questionnaire was sent to some fifty local officials, asking for their opinions of, and experiences with, intergovernmental relations. The responses* made it clear that these local officials are more interested in developing and using intergovernmental collaboration and partnerships than in fine-tuning traditional intergovernmental relations.

The beginnings of this shift from the old hierarchical model of intergovernmental relations (in which cities are at the bottom) to a model based on partnerships, in which officials from all levels of government and the private sector come together as equals to find joint solutions to community problems, were evident from a review of the questionnaires and current practice in many cities and towns. For this reason, the original focus on intergovernmental relations has been augmented with some discussion and examples of intergovernmental collaboration, which may be the highest form of advocacy.

Local officials have a variety of reasons for choosing to become intergovernmental advocates for children and families. While there is

---

* Responses to the intergovernmental questionnaire were received from:

Bloomsburg, Pa.	pop. 11,717
Cambridge, Mass.	pop. 95,322
Fitchburg, Wis.	pop. 15,200
Little Rock, Ark.	pop. 158,915
Los Angeles, Calif.	pop. 2,968,580
Manchester, Ct.	pop. 49,761
Newport News, Va.	pop. 144,903
Oklahoma City, Okla.	pop. 404,014
Owensboro, Ky.	pop. 54,450
Pasadena, Calif.	pop. 118,072
Philadelphia, Pa.	pop. 1,688,210
Pittsburgh, Pa.	pop. 423,959
Rochester, N.Y.	pop. 241,741
Tacoma, Wash.	pop. 158,501
Thornton, Co.	pop. 40,343
Villalba, P. R.	pop. 23,559
League of Iowa Municipalities	

general agreement that the existing system, or maze, of programs and services for children and families isn't working very well, the strategies used to confront it vary. The three major purposes of intergovernmental advocacy are:

■ To **improve** or better use existing programs and services — to do better what is already being done.
■ To **expand** services by increasing the level of resources allocated — to do more of what is already being done.
■ To **reform** or modify the way the systems work — to change the way things are done.

All three are excellent reasons for becoming a more knowledgeable and forceful advocate for the people of your community. Your intergovernmental interests and actions will differ depending on your focus, and you may take a different approach on different issues.

You will find that you sometimes will have to be reactive, like Los Angeles, California, officials were in responding to draft federal child care regulations that would hinder local efforts to increase low-cost after-school care. Or sometimes you can choose to be proactive, like the Oklahoma City officials who actively solicited state legislative changes that improved their police department's ability to help adolescents before they commit criminal offenses.

Depending on your long-range goals, you might be interested in assuring that specific programs are given priority or are expanded in a certain way. But if you are working to integrate a variety of programs for the benefit of a particular population, you will focus your attention more on overall policy questions and linkages at all levels.

Remember that the word advocacy actually means "to speak in favor of, or to plead the cause of another." Even though the federal government uses a term like "Aid to State and Local Government" to refer to most social programs that help people, you don't have to fall into the trap of government-ese. To be most effective, remember that your advocacy isn't on behalf of your city as an institution — you are advocating for the children and families who live in your community.

Chapter One provides the context within which local officials must work: both children and families and the systems that are supposed to be serving them are in crisis.

Chapter Two gives a brief overview of the various government structures which affect children and families and points out opportunities for advocacy in each.

The various ways these intergovernmental pieces fit together to provide particular services to your city's kids are described in **Chapter Three.** Points of flexibility, where local advocacy can be particularly effective, are highlighted in this chapter.

Local efforts to rationalize and coordinate the maze of services and programs are covered in **Chapter Four,** which gives specific examples, resources, and sources for technical assistance.

Chapter Five ties it all together by giving seven key steps to becoming a stronger advocate for your city's kids. These steps are important whether you are already working collaboratively with other entities or you are just beginning a new priority for your city or town.

This guide will give you the kind of information you need in order to decide what you want to do and how you want to do it. The only wrong course of action is not to do anything at all. The children and families of your city or town need your advocacy, and all of us will be the poorer without it.

CHAPTER ONE

The Dual Crises of the 1990s

"The day we decide to approach the problems of our human infrastructure with the same vigor we would use in building a road, we will have made great strides."
Paul Skowron, Town Manager
North Kingstown, Rhode Island.

ocal officials across the country confront dual crises. First, children and families are in crisis. Major demographic, social, and economic changes during the last two decades have converged on our communities and our families, increasing poverty, homelessness, drug and alcohol dependence, and putting every child at risk of not reaching his or her potential. Second, the governmental systems and programs enacted to address the needs of families and children are in crisis. They have become a chaotic and underfunded maze that is fragmented, overlapping, seldom family-centered or reality-based, and often counterproductive.

One of every five children in the United States (and one of every four infants and toddlers) is living in poverty. As a nation, we have the highest unmarried teen pregnancy rate of any industrialized nation, and our infant mortality rate ranks 19th, behind Hong Kong, Spain, and Singapore. Almost two-thirds of married mothers were in the labor force in 1988, yet high quality, affordable child care is unavailable to

many of them. Women with infants make up the fastest growing group in the labor force, but infant care is in short supply in most communities. Economics is one reason why so many mothers are in the work force: the median income of young families with children fell by 26 percent between 1973 and 1989. Every night, 100,000 children are homeless, and every school day, 135,000 American children bring guns to school.[1]

The statistics tell only part of the story and should not be allowed to divert attention from the larger issues.

"Throughout the 1980s, the most profound influence on American families has been the mounting economic pressures which have diminished their resources and made more children vulnerable. The combined effects of persistently high rates of poverty, declining earnings, underemployment, and single parenting have made childhood far more precarious and less safe for millions of America's children. Because these conditions are significantly worse for black and Hispanic families, their children grow up in disproportionately greater jeopardy."[2]

Concerned community and business leaders and elected officials increasingly see the need to respond with both support for families and nurturing guidance for children. They are pushing their local, state, and national governments to strengthen the system of programs sometimes called the "safety net". But they all eventually confront the reality that **there is no system. The programs in place to help children and families constitute the second crisis.**

What exists is a series of narrowly focused, well-meaning programs that offer individual bandaids without the ability to see the scope of the wound. Each has been created to address a particular problem or population, and most are tightly controlled to perform only the function for which they were created. In other words, if a mental health counselor finds out that a client has no food or is about to be evicted, the most he can do is refer the client to another program, which may or may not be able to help.

"The high cost in community comfort and dollar terms of not acting has become clear. The kids hanging on the corner, the crime rate and drug use, concerns about meeting industry's future employment needs and individuals' take-home-pay needs are understood as serious community issues. We meet the needs now or pay much more later."
Alice Wolf, City Councillor and former mayor, Cambridge, Massachusetts

---

In many communities there are families being "served" by five or ten or even more agencies — but with no one responsible for helping them get to the root of their problems. Each one is charged with helping with one symptom — poor grades, child abuse, health needs, under-employment, for instance — but only in rare instances does any one of them have the capacity to look at the whole family, its strengths, weaknesses, and needs. Because the children's needs get dealt with in this fragmented fashion, they are not seen as whole people, but rather as a composite of numerous problems. This is illustrated by the case study of Frank and his family (page 8).

Frank's family's situation also points out that children in your city are affected by policies and programs that originate at all levels of government and are inextricably intertwined.

Recognizing that both our children and families, and the fragmented programs designed to assist them, are in crisis, what should a responsible local government official do?

Sharon Priest, Mayor of Little Rock, Arkansas suggests:

"Because city government usually has the status, clout and ability to make things happen, local elected officials must take the lead in directing cooperative agreements with other governments and in identifying resources. As municipalities gain greater understanding of the fact that our constituents are not constrained by artificial turf boundaries, we will take greater initiative in cooperating with other entities to solve problems common to all of us."[3]

There is, in fact, a growing consensus that local government is best situated to address these dual crises in a humane and effective way. There are several reasons for this emerging point of view:

■ **The issues are more immediate.** "Locally elected people are more responsive to human needs, in part because they don't have to go on a tour or hear about it in an academic discussion. These things are happening right in their neighborhoods," says Phil Hawkey, City Manager of Pasadena, California. The homeless family who sits on the steps of city hall is a clear reminder, both to you and your community, of the failure of many of our systems.

■ **The interconnectedness of the problems is more readily apparent.** When Savannah, Georgia studied crime in the city and its relationship to other factors:

"The study found that the neighborhoods with the highest crime rates and with the highest proportion of criminal offenders were those that had the highest poverty rates, the highest unemployment rates, the highest female-headed household rates, the lowest educational levels, and the lowest neighborhood livability conditions."[4]

Frank's Story

Frank's family may be similar to families in your community.

Frank is a fourteen-year-old who was picked up by city police for selling illegal drugs in front of his home. Because this is the second time he has been arrested, and because the state has decided to get tough on drug pushers, he will likely be sent to the state juvenile detention facility, at a cost to the taxpayer of $26,000 a year.

Frank lives with his mother, who is being treated at a state-funded community mental health clinic for severe depression, his thirteen-year-old sister, and eight-year-old brother. The family receives Aid to Families with Dependent Children (AFDC) and lives in public housing, but has no ongoing relationship with any social worker.

Frank used to play soccer in a league run by the city recreation department. The recreation supervisor had noted that Frank had a lot of potential, but was concerned that he needed male role models and guidance. He talked to the local Big Brother program about Frank, but they didn't have enough volunteers and put him on a waiting list. When Frank stopped coming to the park, no one had time to find out why.

Frank had liked school most of the time and had gotten good grades. But last year he had an English teacher who required oral reading in class. Frank was less able to compensate for his undiagnosed dyslexia when reading aloud, so he refused to do it. This resulted in discipline, which he resisted, and his consequent label as a behavior problem. One day, when he had agreed to read and stumbled over a simple word, a good-looking girl in the class snickered at him. Frank was already becoming well-known on the streets, and at this point decided he could get more respect there than in school. Shortly after this incident, he quit going to school altogether.

Frank's thirteen-year-old sister has begun to skip school and is sexually active. Her relationship with her mother is strained, and they do not communicate well. Last year, one of her teachers had gotten her involved in the school drama program in an effort to build on her interest and talent. But this year the program was dropped because of budget cuts. So, when Frank stopped going to school, she did too.

The eight-year-old is in a half-day special education program at school and spends the other portion of his school days in a day treatment program that specializes in working with children with attention-deficit hyperactivity.

Even given the good intentions of the many professional people working with the individual members of Frank's family, the outlook is not good. No one has ever sat down with all of them together to discuss the interrelatedness of their problems, and how much their living environment is contributing to them, or how they might better support each other and draw on other community resources. Instead, they each will drift through different systems, having their symptoms treated separately, punitively, or not at all.

"Frank's" story is a composite of two actual case histories, with the names and certain other details changed to protect confidentiality.

Savannah's leaders knew that they could not solve all of these problems alone, so they created an intergovernmental Youth Futures Authority, which is described in detail on page 48 in Chapter Four.

■ **They are already involved.** Cities realize that they already are providing many services to children and their families through their traditional services. The police department plays a role in serving abused and neglected children; the library is affected by "latchkey" children; and many local governments provide health services. In addition, cities play an important role in authorizing, prohibiting, or enabling other service providers through such functions as licensing, zoning, and inspection. Because they already are major actors in the field, cities have a real stake in improving the effectiveness of services.

■ **The scope of the problems is more manageable.** Reformers at other levels of government run into formidable barriers when they try to change entire systems. Cities can choose to focus on a particular geographic area or other target population and bring together all the service systems around a set of common goals, without trying to attack all the ills of the systems at once.

■ **Local business is directly affected.** The results of our failures are readily apparent to local businesses. They may not be able to find enough entry-level high school graduates with the skills they need, or they may have their buildings defaced by graffiti or vandalism. Local business people often are also parents

with a personal stake in the improvement of conditions for all children and families. They are more likely to become a part of the local solution than to be involved at other levels. In Chicago, for example, local business leaders were some of the strongest advocates for school reform, and they helped lobby the state legislature for its passage.

Many cities already have begun to take a leadership role in improving conditions and outcomes for children. Many more are realizing that the future of their community depends on improving the chances of success for their children and that they cannot look to other levels of government for the kind of leadership that is needed. From Cambridge, Massachusetts, to Tacoma, Washington, and Ft. Worth, Texas,

---

"Communities must begin to see children and family support services as essential to the success of other goals such as economic development, quality education and revitalization of urban areas. Children and families are the foundation upon which these goals must be developed." Thomas P. Ryan, Mayor, Rochester, New York.

---

cities are taking action. The May 1990 issue of *Public Management,* published by the International City Management Association (ICMA), was devoted entirely to "The 1990s Priority: Managing Our Human Infrastructure Needs." At the National League of Cities (NLC), the Task Force on the Future of Youth in America's Cities and Towns has recommended that NLC include children and youth as the top priority for action on its national agenda. The NLC Board of Directors established children and families as one of seven priorities for 1992 at its March 1992 meeting. The NLC Advisory Council is devoting its 1992 Futures Process to the topic of family-friendly cities and towns.

If you wish to join this movement and work to improve conditions for the children and families in your community, you need to understand the national, state, and local structures that exist to provide services or resources for them. With that knowledge, you will be better prepared to hold government accountable, to assure that your community is making the best possible use of all available resources, and to take action to improve, expand, or reform those resources. An understanding of the types of strategies that your colleagues around the country are trying will also be important to you. In the next three chapters, we will give you both.

Notes

1. Figures taken from Children's Defense Fund, *An Opinion Maker's Guide to Children in Election Year 1992* and *The State of America's Children 1991,* Washington D.C. 1991, and *Children 1990: A Report Card, Briefing Book, and Action Primer,* Washington, D.C. 1990.
2. Select Committee On Children, Youth and Families. *U.S. Children and Their Families: Current Conditions and Recent Trends, 1989, p. x,* U.S. House of Representatives, Washington, D.C. 1989.
3. Priest, Sharon. Response to NLC questionnaire, September, 1991.
4. Mendonsa, Arthur A. (Don). "Underclass Families: The Challenge We Must Meet" p. 5 in *Public Management,* International City Management Association, Washington, D.C., May, 1990.

CHAPTER TWO

Who Does What To Whom?

A brief review of the national, state, and local systems and how they operate programs for children and families.

Our federal system of government was set out in the Constitution to assure that no single aspect of government could become all-powerful. Through a series of compromises, the framers of the Constitution divided authority between the national and state governments and split the national government into three independent branches — executive, legislative, and judicial.

The Constitution grants the national government certain expressed and implied powers, such as the right to collect taxes, declare war, and regulate trade. All powers not granted explicitly or implicitly to the federal government or specifically prohibited to the states are reserved to the states or the people. In some areas, such as protecting the health and welfare of the people, the national and state governments are granted concurrent powers — that is, both may act in these areas.

Because local government is not mentioned in the Constitution, the states have the authority to create and to control various units of local government. Of course, each state has used this power to create a local governmental infrastructure that is particularly suited to its history, traditions, politics, and needs — and no two states are exactly alike.

Thus, the seeds of the chaotic system that has blossomed over time were planted in the Constitution itself in order to assure that power was shared among the levels of government in the fledgling republic. One intergovernmental observer describes it as "a system of blurred accountability and overall blame shifting, where no one is exclusively responsible for anything, and everyone can blame everyone else for almost everything."[1]

Intergovernmental relations — that is, the ways in which governments interact — have, like many other things, become more complex over time. Discussions of intergovernmental relations often focus on vertical interactions among federal, state, and local governments. But horizontal relations, among separate governments at the same level (such as city-county, among adjacent towns, or between school district and city), are also important.

During most of the first two centuries of our history, the state, national, and local governments had fairly distinct roles. While all were involved, to some extent, in providing education, health and human services, interaction was limited.

Toward the middle of this century, there was a growing federal concern that many states were not adequately meeting the health and welfare needs of the people. During the 1960s, therefore, the federal government began to offer states and local governments significant financial incentives to join it in funding and providing new community and human service programs. For a relatively small matching amount, states and municipalities could draw on substantial federal funds to provide specific services to their residents. Beyond the financial matching requirements, these new funds were accompanied by explicit guidelines on how they were to be used to meet the national goals as set by the Congress and the President. They also necessitated a new and more intense kind of intergovernmental relationship between state and local officials and the federal government.

As these intergovernmental domestic programs expanded and multiplied, some were channeled through the states, while others flowed directly from the federal government to local governments. Some by-passed state and local governments altogether when the federal program provided direct funding to local non-profit organizations. The effects of the complex new partnerships and intergovernmental linkages were many. In both state and local governments, as services to assist communities and individuals grew, so too did federal control over certain programmatic, fiscal and governance questions.[2]

In the 1970s and early 1980s, a commitment developed to reverse this trend — both in terms of federal financial assistance and federal control. While some steps had been taken earlier, Ronald Reagan's first budget as President (the Omnibus Budget Reconciliation Act of 1981) was the first major act implementing this "New Federalism". According to an analysis done by Richard Cole, it "resulted in the consolidation of seventy-seven categorical grants into nine block grants. In contrast to existing block grants whose funds mainly went directly to local governments, the Reagan-supported block grants reassigned program funding and control exclusively to the states, [while at the same time reducing the amount available]. Over the full period of the Reagan Presidency, federal spending on grants to state and local governments declined by over 10 percent."[3] At the same time, responsibility for programs was shifted in the name of "local control."

From the perspective of local governments, the two most important results of the New Federalism were the loss of direct federal revenues and the increased need for strong working relationships with state government because of its increased involvement and flexibility in administering federal funds. Cole's study concluded that "large proportions of cities in all size and regional categories have had to significantly trim service deliveries" and that "the evidence indicates that the burdens of New Federalism have been felt most by those in the lower and moderate income groups." These are, of course, the very people who are turning to local government to help meet their needs.

In other words, municipalities are faced with more responsibility and fewer resources to meet the needs of their citizens. New and creative intergovernmental partnerships and stronger advocacy must be developed to meet those needs in this transition period.

To assist you as you consider your role as an intergovernmental advocate, the next few pages will give an overview of the national, state, and local governmental structures that affect services or resources for children and families, and highlight key points where your advocacy can be most effective.

The Federal Government

As we all know, the federal government is divided into three branches. The legislative branch, or Congress, enacts the laws, the executive branch implements the laws, and the judicial branch interprets the laws and settles disagreements between the other two branches. All three affect the children and families of your community, and all three are appropriate targets of different types of intergovernmental advocacy.

The Legislative Branch

Congress meets in two-year sessions, which are organized after the November elections of each even-numbered year. The sessions have been consecutively numbered since the first in 1789-1791. The members who were elected in November of 1990 formed the 102nd Congress.

Both the House of Representatives and the Senate have numerous committees and subcommittees, which hold hearings on specific topics and generate new legislation and amendments to existing laws. They also provide oversight to certain federal programs. It is important to know on which committees your local representatives serve, and which programs come under the jurisdiction of those committees. Members often develop expertise in the areas of their committee assignments and become particularly influential in those areas.

In fact, the committee structure itself is one of the factors that has led us into the categorical and fragmented system of services we currently have. Each committee and subcommittee guards its program turf jealously. Important social programs and long legislative careers are sometimes built on the basis of a member's strong committee work in a particular field. Keeping the program narrowly focused allows elected officials to spread the credit for responding to particular aspects of a problem and assures that the money is used exactly as the committee intended. Coordination of services does not have as much political appeal as developing a new program for a photogenic client group, even if it might help them more in the long run.

Congress, through its committee structure, tends to create narrowly defined categorical programs, tied to a particular constituent group and a particular committee and requiring a specific bureaucratic structure to implement.

The resulting three-sided advocacy force for the program has sometimes been called the "iron triangle" and can become very influential. Anyone wishing to affect or change an existing program must be aware of the members of its iron triangle — that is, the congressional or state legislative subcommittees with jurisdiction over the program, the federal or state agencies responsible for administering it, and the national, state, or local constituent groups that are affected by it.

A continually up-dated listing of the congressional committees and subcommittees, their members, and the programs over which they have jurisdiction is published by the Congressional Quarterly in the *Congressional Yellow Book*, which is available at most large libraries.

If you have a specific question or need information, a good place to start is the House Select Committee on Children, Youth and Families, H2-385, House Office Building Annex

2, Washington, D.C. 20515; (202) 226-7660. As a select committee, rather than an authorizing committee, this body does not pass legislation. It studies the conditions of children, youth, and families and the programs that affect them and makes recommendations to other committees. It is the one place in Congress where the needs of families and children can be viewed in their entirety. If a member of Congress from your area is on the Select Committee, be sure to establish a relationship with him or her and get to know the staff people involved with the issues of importance to you.

Speaking of staff, you should be aware of the critical role played by staff in most Congressional actions. No single human being can personally keep up with all of the issues that come before Congress during a session, so members depend on their professional staffs to review the issues and advise them on the options. Each Senator and Representative is authorized to staff a district office (or offices) as well as a Washington office.

The staff members in the district office are usually local people who are skilled at working with constituents and local officials, such as you and your city council. They may be very helpful in gaining support for local projects and in scheduling time with the Congress member.

Depending on the issues you are concerned about and the level of involvement you wish to have, it can also be very helpful to connect with the specific Washington staff person who works in your area of interest. Congressional staff people can be excellent sources of information and contacts both on legislative matters and in the executive branch. And they are generally interested in the way legislation affects the people in the district. Over time, you may become one of the people with whom the staff confers before advising the member on a vote.

Each of the committees and subcommittees also has a cadre of professional staff members who are experts in the areas of the committee's jurisdiction and serve members of both parties.

Of course, nothing takes the place of a close working relationship between elected officials, but don't neglect the potential benefits of strong relationships with staff members as well.

The Executive Branch

The House Select Committee on Children, Youth and Families has identified 125 federal programs in ten departments and two independent agencies that directly affect or respond to the needs of children and their families. Figure I is an organizational chart of the executive branch showing the various departments and major programs for children and families. Each department has regional offices, and each has an Office of Intergovernmental Relations. These offices are usually very helpful and will respond to your needs for information or assistance.

The executive branch department that administers the largest number of programs for children and families is the Department of Health and Human Services (HHS). In April 1991, HHS announced a reorganization of its operating divisions which "places greater emphasis and greater focus on the needs of America's children and families."[4] The Administration for Children and Families (ACF) was created by combining the major divisions that had responsibility for children's and family programs and income support. Among the programs now administered by ACF are the Social Services Block Grant, Maternal and Child Health Block Grant, Aid to Families with Dependent Children (AFDC), Job Opportunities and Basic Skills (JOBS), Child Welfare Services and Adoption Assistance, Foster Care, Child Care and Development Block Grant, and Head Start.

The effects of this reorganization on your city or town will probably not be monumental. It may, however, simplify your relations with the HHS regional office nearest you. (There are ten across the country.) The regional administrator for ACF becomes a focal point for issues relating to many of the major programs for children and families. Each regional ACF also has an Office of Public Affairs, which is a useful contact when you need assistance or information. There may be some tangible benefits of the reorganization, as well. One federal official acknowledged that the consolidation of responsibility for all of these programs had already brought to light some inconsistent policies within HHS. "We actually have policies in different programs which are working against each other, and that will be easier to remedy now," she explained.

Figure 1
Major Executive Branch Programs for Children & Families

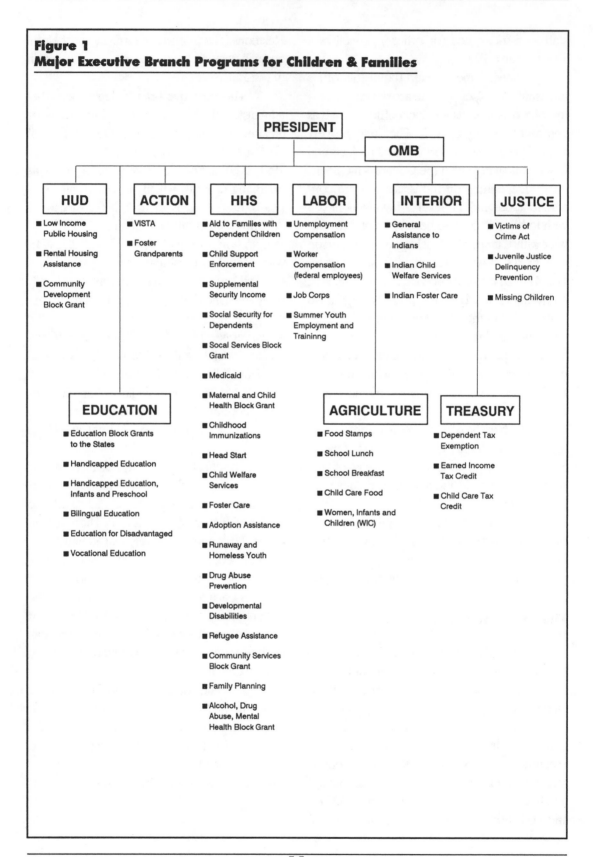

PRESIDENT

OMB

HUD
- Low Income Public Housing
- Rental Housing Assistance
- Community Development Block Grant

ACTION
- VISTA
- Foster Grandparents

HHS
- Aid to Families with Dependent Children
- Child Support Enforcement
- Supplemental Security Income
- Social Security for Dependents
- Socal Services Block Grant
- Medicaid
- Maternal and Child Health Block Grant
- Childhood Immunizations
- Head Start
- Child Welfare Services
- Foster Care
- Adoption Assistance
- Runaway and Homeless Youth
- Drug Abuse Prevention
- Developmental Disabilities
- Refugee Assistance
- Community Services Block Grant
- Family Planning
- Alcohol, Drug Abuse, Mental Health Block Grant

LABOR
- Unemployment Compensation
- Worker Compensation (federal employees)
- Job Corps
- Summer Youth Employment and Traininng

INTERIOR
- General Assistance to Indians
- Indian Child Welfare Services
- Indian Foster Care

JUSTICE
- Victims of Crime Act
- Juvenile Justice Delinquency Prevention
- Missing Children

EDUCATION
- Education Block Grants to the States
- Handicapped Education
- Handicapped Education, Infants and Preschool
- Bilingual Education
- Education for Disadvantaged
- Vocational Education

AGRICULTURE
- Food Stamps
- School Lunch
- School Breakfast
- Child Care Food
- Women, Infants and Children (WIC)

TREASURY
- Dependent Tax Exemption
- Earned Income Tax Credit
- Child Care Tax Credit

Administrative Advocacy

Many people think of advocacy chiefly in terms of influencing legislative bodies. Administrative or policy advocacy is also a very important part of intergovernmental relations. Executive agencies write implementing regulations, distribute grants, develop demonstration projects, administer programs, and determine who receives waivers. All of these functions can be critical to the improvement of conditions in your community, so they deserve your attention.

Once a law is passed and signed by the President, an executive branch agency becomes responsible for its implementation. Usually, the first thing the agency will do is draft a set of regulations designed to govern the program.

When adopted in final form, regulations have the force of law, and they determine how programs will operate at the local level. It is important that they accurately reflect both the intent of Congress and, to the extent possible, the realities and needs of your community. Under the Administrative Procedures Act, proposed regulations are published in the *Federal Register* and the public is given an opportunity to comment, usually a period of thirty to ninety days. Each individual letter is counted, reviewed, and taken into consideration as the draft rules are revised. Comments from an elected official about the potential impact of proposed regulations can be particularly influential — especially if you state the local case clearly and offer positive suggestions. Always send a copy of your comments to your members of Congress. They may use them in developing their own responses.

How do you know when there are regulations you should comment on? Certainly you won't want to read through hundreds of pages of the *Federal Register* every week. To help you, you can cultivate connections in three areas: (1) the state and local advocacy networks in your areas of interest; (2) Congressional staff with whom you worked on relevant legislation; and (3) the regional office of the relevant federal department. Chapter Five provides more detailed information about establishing such connections.

If you are eager to read the *Federal Register* for yourself, it can be found in every government depository library (there is at least one in every congressional district) and in many other local public libraries.

The Judicial Branch

The judicial branch was created to interpret the laws and to resolve differences between the other two branches. It is mentioned in this book on intergovernmental advocacy, not because anyone would suggest lobbying a court in the traditional sense, but because turning to the courts is sometimes the only way to get your issue addressed.

For example, several cities banded together in 1991 to sue the Census Bureau after their documentation of a significant undercount had not been acted upon. Since many federal programs are based on the population figures published in the census, and since the undercounted populations tend to be poor families, this suit could have a major impact on the children and families in those cities and others.

Cities may also wish to consider filing supportive briefs in court cases brought by other parties which affect their community. For example, law suits brought by advocates on behalf of children with disabilities were crucial in holding the federal government accountable for providing Supplemental Security Income (SSI) benefits to everyone who is entitled to them. This issue probably affected many people in your community, and its positive resolution has likely enhanced their quality of life. As a result, children with physical or mental impairments who were denied SSI benefits may now be eligible. They may even be owed benefits, even if they are now adults. You can call (800) 772-1213 for more information.

A Resource

The U.S. Advisory Commission on Intergovernmental Relations is an important resource for all governmental officials interested in improving intergovernmental functioning. It was created by Congress in 1959 to monitor the operation of the American federal system and to recommend improvements. It is a permanent, national, bipartisan body representing the executive and legislative branches of federal, state, and local government and the public. The current local government members include four mayors and three elected county officials.

ACIR does research on issues of intergovernmental interest, and publishes a quarterly magazine, *Intergovernmental Perspective*. A list of publications or other information can be obtained from the Commission at: U.S. ACIR, Suite 450, Tech World, South Building, 800 K St. NW, Washington, D.C. 20575. Telephone: (202) 653-5640.

State Government

The fifty state governments all mirror the three branches of the federal government, with the exception of Nebraska which has a unicameral (one chamber) legislature. Virtually all of the advocacy opportunities in the federal government have a counterpart at the state level.

State Legislatures

State legislatures vary greatly in size and staffing. Seven states, such as Massachusetts, have full-time legislatures that have full-time professional staffs for both members and committees. Many state legislatures have few staff and meet for a limited session of sixty or ninety days each year. Some meet only every other year. At least seventeen of the legislatures have Committees on Children and Families or Children and Youth. Your local legislator's office is the best place to find out the specifics about your state legislature's organization. The personal staff of elected members and committee staff people, where they exist, are also excellent sources of information.

Twenty-nine states now have some kind of Advisory Commission on Intergovernmental Relations, and the number is growing. A Task Force of the National Conference of State Legislatures (NCSL) recommended in 1989 that:

"Each state needs an organization dedicated to studying state-local issues and resolving problems, either a state advisory commission on intergovernmental relations or a legislative commission on state-local relations. It should be created by statute, have strong legislative representation, and have adequate budget and staff."[5]

The kind of independent commission envisioned by this task force includes representation from the state legislature and executive branch, as well as local governments. The task force members suggest that it should conduct research, provide a forum for discussion and development of recommendations on long-term state-local issues, promote experimentation in intergovernmental processes, and act as an ombudsman for local governments which are having difficulty with state agencies.

If there is such a commission in your state, it could be helpful in drawing attention to the systemic issues facing local governments that are trying to improve services for the children and families in their communities. Find out who represents the cities and discuss the possibility of making these issues a priority agenda item. Maybe you or someone else from your city council would like to serve on it. Your state municipal league (the organization serving as the advocate for municipal government in your state) can give you information.

Another important recommendation of the NCSL Task Force on State-Local Relations is that "each state reevaluate its system of 'sorting out' responsibilities in view of the new fiscal environment." The recommendation goes on to say that "states should take a step toward rationalizing the intergovernmental system that has developed incrementally over time, often with confusing results."[6] This puts you in good company when you make the same points. You are not alone.

The Executive Branch

The state executive branches vary as well. Many governors have created special offices for children and youth to advise the governor and monitor state programs and policies. In at least fourteen states, children's commissions have been created either by the governor or legislature.

In Oklahoma, for example, the legislature created a Commission on Children and Youth in 1982 and gave it a strong oversight role, including inspections of state and private facilities. If your state has such a commission, or is contemplating one, be sure to ask that local government be represented on it. Or work through your state municipal league to assure that the vital, local aspects of the problems and solutions are recognized.

Most states issue proposed regulations for public comment. Some have laws similar to the federal Administrative Procedures Act; others issue regulations through the governor's office or the office of the attorney general. Again, your state municipal league can give you information on your state's procedures, and local or state advocates, advocacy groups, state legislators, or program officials can notify you about pending regulations of special interest.

State Administrative Systems

State service systems can be as complex as the federal systems. In a 1990 study, the National Conference of State Legislatures surveyed the state systems which serve children in crisis. Specifically, they reviewed the ways states deliver four types of services: child welfare services for abused, neglected, and dependent children; juvenile justice services for delinquents; youth services for status offenders (non-criminal children in need of supervision — truants, runaways, and incorrigibles, for example — are status offenders); and mental health services for emotionally disturbed children. Among the findings of this study are the following:

> "The survey confirmed that most state service systems are intricate, complicated networks combining a variety of service delivery approaches and organizational structures, with little inter-system coordination.

> "Almost two-thirds of the states operate through multiple, autonomous agencies, each of which is responsible for services to one or more designated populations. These multiple, autonomous agencies are often fragmented, uncoordinated, and competitive and have special difficulty responding to children and families with multiple problems.

Figure 2
State Agency Structures Serving Children and Youth in Crisis

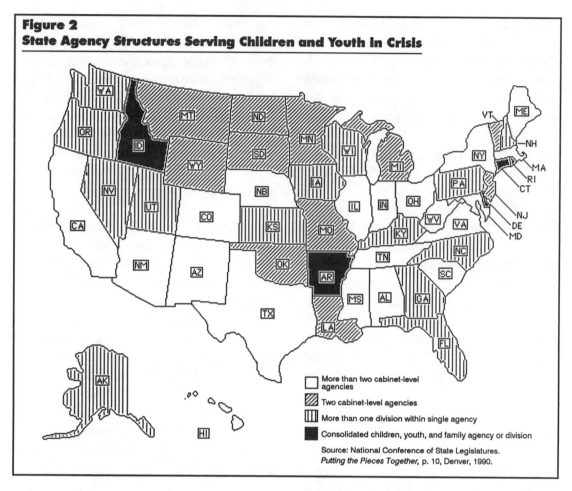

More than two cabinet-level agencies

Two cabinet-level agencies

More than one division within single agency

Consolidated children, youth, and family agency or division

Source: National Conference of State Legislatures.
Putting the Pieces Together, p. 10, Denver, 1990.

"Inadequate fiscal resources were reported by a significant number of states...at the same time, inflexible, categorical funding streams are considered a significant barrier to delivering services effectively in a majority of states. **Financing systems determine services, rather than the needs of children and families.**"[7]

The last sentence of this quotation underscores the fact that the budget is the most important policy document at any level of government. These findings also emphasize the complexity of the job of an intergovernmental advocate or service provider who wishes to take a holistic approach to children's and family services.

The map in Figure 2 (above) shows how many agencies are involved in providing these services in each state. If you are lucky enough to live in Idaho, Connecticut, Arkansas, Rhode Island, or Delaware, you have a single agency to work with at the state level on this group of services.

Local Governments

As mentioned earlier, local governments are legally created and regulated by the states — even when they functionally pre-date the state government, as do many eastern cities. State legislatures have created, or permitted the creation of, several types of local government entities. Counties, cities, towns, townships, and school districts are the most common, but in some states there are also special districts governed by elected library boards or parks and recreation commissions.

In Florida, county voters can choose to create a special taxing authority specifically for children's services. The oldest and best known of these, the Juvenile Welfare Board of Pinellas County (St. Petersburg), is described on page 36 in Chapter Three.

County Government

Forty-eight states are divided into county governments (called "boroughs" in Alaska and "parishes" in Louisiana). Connecticut and Rhode Island have no functional county governments. Altogether, there are more than 3,000 counties in the country, and another 22 city-county consolidations like Philadelphia, San Francisco, and Jacksonville. There are eight states that have fewer than 20 counties; Texas, in contrast, has 254. County populations range from less than two hundred people in Loving County, Texas, to almost nine million (and eighty-seven cities) in Los Angeles County, California.

The functions performed by the counties vary as much as their size. They were created primarily to serve as administrative arms of the state, but most have also become the "municipal" government for the populations of unincorporated areas, providing law enforcement, courts, road maintenance, and other services. In some states, like Minnesota and California, counties are responsible for the administration of many state and federally funded programs and services, such as AFDC and Foster Care. In others, like Texas and Utah, counties do not play a large role in the delivery of human services.

In most counties, elected board members or commissioners serve as both the legislative body and head of the executive branch. Fewer than 400 counties have separately elected executives to mirror the separation of powers and accountability of the state and federal governments. Historically, this has been generally acceptable given the traditional county role as agent of the state. But this arrangement has caused some concern in states where county governments have become almost as complex as states. Los Angeles County, for example, is now responsible for the delivery of almost all state and federal human services (and an annual budget of $11 billion), but is still governed by a five-member board with both executive and legislative powers and no elected chief executive. On the other hand, Orange County, Florida (Orlando) — one of the more recent counties to change — elected its first county executive in November 1990.[8]

Cities, Towns and Villages

Historically, the mission of municipal government in this country was the preservation of public health and public safety. Traditional municipal departments such as fire, police, public works, inspections, parks and recreation, and public health came into being to carry out this mission. The movement to bring city government back into the forefront of the provision of human services does not constitute a new role for cities.

It is vitally important for today's cities and towns to understand that they play many roles that affect the lives of children and families. Municipal governments can take a proactive stance to improve conditions for children and families by carrying out their traditional functions with that focus in mind. Here are some examples of traditional city functions and some ways they can be used to improve conditions and services for children and families:

■ Regulate — zoning and building permits can encourage attention to children's needs, e.g., for play space or child care.

■ Tax — tax and fee policies can encourage businesses and developers to address community priorities.

■ Exercise police powers — community-based policing might enhance neighborhood life through a personal, preventive focus.

■ Exert intergovernmental influence — help set the agenda by serving on intergovernmental bodies and commenting on state plans and regulations.

■ Serve as a model employer — devise municipal personnel policies that include parental leave, flexible hours, child care assistance, and incentives to volunteer.

■ Influence local business decisions — suggest that businesses provide release time for parent-teacher conferences or tutoring, and lead by example.

■ Purchase goods and services — give preference to vendors with strong family-oriented policies or to those that train or hire local youth.

■ Provide public and political leadership — keep children's issues highly visible.

■ Facilitate community action and problem solving — convene community meetings around issues of importance.

■ Provide services directly — assure that all local government staff who work with children are trained in child development.

■ Make grants — give high priority to collaborative, interagency proposals.

■ Coordinate and facilitate the provision of services by others — act as a resource and referral agent and/or as an intergovernmental and case advocate on behalf of residents.

■ Appoint members of advisory and planning bodies — add strong child and family advocacy to the criteria required for appointments to the planning and zoning commissions and other boards and committees.

■ Participate in regional Councils of Governments — use such bodies to meet cross-cutting issues such as providing regional transportation systems that can focus on children's needs to get to school and to after-school recreation.

Sid Gardner, a former Hartford, Connecticut, city council member, has spent a lifetime working on these issues and is now consulting with a variety of organizations and cities on collaborative projects. He points out that cities' intergovernmental relations often are defensive and reactive. This stems, in large part, from the reality that their choice of revenue sources and their legal self-determination are at the mercy of other levels of government. Cities are closest to the people and the problems, but they have the worst tax and revenue base. So they, quite naturally, respond defensively — trying to assure that shifts of responsibility and new mandates don't harm their position any further. But, remembering that the best defense is a good offense, Gardner urges cities to develop their own strategies, rather than simply responding to someone else's. Chapter Five describes some specific steps to take in developing your own intergovernmental agenda.

The Private Not-For-Profit Sector

While this is a guide to intergovernmental programming and advocacy, it is important to include a discussion of the not-for-profit agencies through whom many government-funded services are delivered. "Contracting out" is not a new idea in the field of human services. Government has been contracting with private agencies for decades to house, clothe, and feed abandoned children; to care for the children of employed mothers; and to provide a variety of family services. As you look at your community's systems (or non-systems) of services for children and families, you may wish to inventory all of the private sector agencies that provide services. An aggregation of their annual budgets may well show that they are raising and spending more for children and family services than the city itself is. The members of their boards of directors may also make powerful advocacy partners for you. One of your community's greatest strengths may be well-established private organizations with histories of service and fund-raising and advocacy capacities of their own. There may also be new, young, and vital agencies with energy and connections that can help the cause. Of course, you may also have your share of agencies that are stuck in the myopic view that their responsibility is to the agency, rather than to community needs. But government cannot do the job alone — so remember to include private sector agencies in your planning and advocacy.

Service organizations are another aspect of the not-for-profit sector that can play a role in both advocacy and improving services. For example, Kiwanis International has adopted a three-year major emphasis program called "Young Children: Priority One." Each Kiwanis Club has been provided with information and program ideas about how it can help to address the needs of children, prenatal through age five.

In Lynchburg, Virginia, the Kiwanis Club is working with the public health department in an innovative two-year program to achieve 100 percent immunization of two-year-olds by September 1992. In Bradenton, Florida, Kiwanis responded to news of a 500-child waiting list for day care by acquiring and renovating a building for a new day care center. The Kiwanis Club of Burlington, Wisconsin, sponsored a parenting fair that drew 2,300 people and provided workshops and a screening service for young children with disabilities.

These are just a few examples of the kinds of projects that have been undertaken. The options are limited only by the number of people in your local service organizations and your collective imagination and drive.

Notes

1. Gardner, Sid (Former city council member, Hartford, Connecticut). Personal interview, September, 1991.
2. Banovetz, James M. *Small Cities and Counties: A Guide To Managing Services*, International City Management Association, Washington, D.C., 1984.
3. Cole, R., Hissong, R. and Taebel, D. "America's Cities and the 1980s: A Legacy of the Reagan Years," *Journal of Urban Affairs*, Volume 12, Number 4, 1990.
4. U.S. Department of Health and Human Services. "Announcement of Reorganization of Operating Divisions," Washington, D. C., 1991.
5. Gold, S. *Reforming State-Local Relations: A Practical Guide*, National Conference of State Legislatures, Washington, D.C., 1989.
6. ibid.
7. Robison, S. *Putting The Pieces Together: Survey of State Systems For Children in Crisis*, National Conference of State Legislatures, Washington, D.C., 1990.

8. Jeffery, B., Salant, T., and Boroshok, A. *County Government Structure*, National Association of Counties, Washington, D.C., 1989.

CHAPTER THREE

How the Intergovernmental Pieces Fit Together

For the advocate for children and families, the various levels and units of government can sometimes seem like a gigantic jig-saw puzzle. Here's how the pieces fit together.

The intergovernmental flow of programs, resources, and services differs from state to state and from program to program. It is, therefore, impossible to provide a single set of guidelines to help all local officials assure that their communities are taking full advantage of available resources. Instead, this chapter describes the ways the pieces of the intergovernmental puzzle fit together, shows where flexibility exists, and gives you some pointers on specific questions to ask and examples of how other municipalities are making the best of the chaotic maze on behalf of their children and families.

Entitlement or Appropriation?

Programs are either **entitlements** or they are subject to the **appropriations** process.

The Congressional Budget Office defines entitlement programs as "programs that make payments to any person, business, or unit of government that seeks the payment and meets the criteria set in law. The Congress thus controls spending for these programs indirectly, by defining eligibility and setting the benefit or payment rules, rather than directly through the appropriations process."[1]

In an **entitlement** program, any individual or unit of government that meets program eligibility rules is **entitled** to program benefits. Of the 125 programs identified by the House Select Committee on Children, Youth and Families as serving children and families, 31 are entitlements. Anyone who is eligible under the rules must be given Aid to Families with Dependent Children (AFDC) benefits, Food Stamps, Social Security, Unemployment Compensation, Medicaid, and the Earned Income Tax Credit, for example. The only way to control the costs of an entitlement program is to change

the level of benefits, or the rules governing who is eligible for the program. In 1981, for example, the AFDC program budget was cut by reducing the amount of outside income an eligible person could earn. This eliminated many "working poor" families from the entitlement and reduced projected expenditures.

Most federal programs are not entitlements and are subject to the **appropriations** process. This means that regardless of the amount **authorized** by Congress to be spent on the program, it must compete in the appropriations process each year. The program will receive a finite amount of money, beyond which it may not spend. Most social service, education and training, health, and housing programs are subject to the appropriations process in Congress. The Women, Infants and Children (WIC) nutrition program and Head Start are not entitlements; they can serve only the number of people for which funds are appropriated each year. In 1991, WIC served about 60 percent of those who were eligible, and Head Start had funding to serve fewer than one in three eligible children.[2]

This question of entitlement can be an important policy factor. For example, the Foster Care Program, which is jointly funded by federal, state, and (in some instances) county governments, is an entitlement. Any child who has been abused or neglected, and cannot be left safely in his or her family, is entitled to foster care placement, which the program will pay for in full. On the other hand, the Title IV-B Child Welfare Services program of preventive and pre-placement services is subject to the appropriations process and has never been fully funded to provide needed services for all eligible children. The result is a system that pays the full cost of out-of-home placement for eligible children but underfunds the support services that could help some of those families stay together and avoid placement.

These budget decisions have direct program implications. In a 1990 study, The National Commission on Child Welfare and Family Preservation found that "public child welfare nationally focuses narrowly on five services" which are basically crisis-oriented, while "intensive home-based services and respite services are the lowest on the list of forty possible services in terms of statewide availability." The study goes on to state that "preventive services are seriously underrepresented among the standard services offered by public child welfare agencies."[3]

This highlights an issue that all policy makers must face as they make budget decisions, and it suggests good questions to ask about all program and budget decisions. Does this policy (or grant or appropriation) support crisis-oriented services without examining the need for prevention efforts? Are we working against preventing problems by dealing only with the symptoms and not the causes of those problems?

There are seven basic ways that public programs for children and families are provided:

- direct federal benefits;
- federal programs delivered through a local contractor or grantee;
- federal-local government programs;
- federal-state-local partnerships;
- state-local programs;
- locally generated programs; and
- interlocal or municipal/school district programs.

Each offers its own opportunities for local advocacy.

1. Direct Federal Benefits

Detailed information on the 125 federal programs that serve children and families is published periodically by the House Select Committee on Children, Youth and Families. According to their report, *Federal Programs Affecting Children and Their Families, 1990,* about 15 percent of these programs, which represent "by far, most of the value of benefits", are administered by federal agencies, with benefits going directly to children and their families. These benefits include Social Security, Supplemental Security Income (SSI), and benefits for special populations such as military personnel, veterans, and Native Americans.[4]

They also include the Earned Income Credit (EIC), which offers cash aid to working parents who earn less than $20,000 and have a dependent child. The EIC is a refundable tax credit, which means that if the family does not owe any taxes, or owes less in taxes than the credit they are eligible for, the IRS pays them the difference. For example, a family with an adjusted gross income under $10,730 received $953 in 1990. Thanks to legislation passed by the

1990 Congress, this amount will increase steadily through 1994. Families need not owe any tax to receive the credit, but they must apply for it by filing income tax returns. A family can also file an earned income eligibility certificate with the employer to receive advance payment of the credit.[5]

Because many low-income families are not in the habit of filing income tax returns, and because the availability of the EIC is not well known in some communities, local outreach efforts in some areas have been successful in helping eligible families receive these benefits to which they are entitled. This might be an easy way to begin your family-centered advocacy, perhaps in conjunction with your local member of congress. Mayor Elihu Harris of Oakland, California, working with a coalition of community groups, spearheaded an outreach and education effort in 1991, by declaring March 15 to April 15 as Earned Income Credit Month. He estimated that approximately 55,000 Oakland families were due a total of between $15 million and $40 million.

2. Federal-Local Grantee

In about 40 percent of the programs affecting children and their families, the federal agencies make grants directly to local public and private agencies, such as local government, community agencies, or schools. Head Start is a good example of this kind of federal-local program, in which state and local governments are completely by-passed unless they happen to apply to become the grantee themselves.

Head Start provides educational, health, and social services to preschool children whose families meet low-income eligibility requirements. There is some flexibility in the design of the specific program provided by each grantee. Local decisions include such questions as: Will

it be a half-day preschool program or a full day program including day care? (About 80 percent of the programs are half-day.) Will the program run year-round or only during the regular school year?

One of the goals of the program is parent involvement and leadership development. Each program site has a parent council, and each grantee (which may administer numerous sites) has a Parent Policy Council (PPC), which is given, by law and regulation, power to approve or veto agency budgets and program decisions. The PPC must be involved in all major decisions affecting the administration and development of the program. This is a powerful empowerment tool, and it also offers an opportunity for the development of close working relations. Each PPC can appoint a number of community representatives who are not Head Start parents, but represent other aspects of the community. This provides an opportunity for your city to become involved in a supportive way at the grassroots level — and to have some input on how the federal funds are used. You might suggest that an appropriate city official or staff member offer to serve in this capacity.

In Pasadena, California, the Pasadena Head Start PPC includes staff persons from the local school district and the city government as community representatives. While there is no requirement for local government representation, it has worked to the advantage of everyone involved to build in this type of coordination.

3. Federal-Local Government

While most of the direct aid from the federal government to local communities was ended during the 1980s, the Community Development Block Grant (CDBG) continues to provide formula grants to localities directed toward neighborhood revitalization, economic development, and/or improved community facilities and services. It is designed to benefit primarily low- and moderate-income people. CDBG funds are also available to reimburse the city for the costs associated with administering the program.

All metropolitan areas with populations greater than 50,000 are entitled to their share of these funds. The municipal governments of cities and towns with populations smaller than 50,000 can apply for the funds through the Small Cities CDBG program, which is administered by each state.

In this time of shrinking resources for services, this program, known mostly for its funding of "bricks and mortar" projects, has a useful, but not well-known provision. Cities may set aside up to 15 percent of their grant to be used for social services such as child care, youth services, and job training. Binghamton, New York, uses some of its CDBG money to contract with local non-profit child care providers to help low- and very-low-income families. Santa Ana, California, uses CDBG money to help fund a mobile elementary school health van that provides medical assistance in the city's neediest schools. Some advocates believe that the limit should be increased from 15 percent to 25 percent to give local officials more flexibility in meeting local needs.

The Small Cities CDBG programs, which are administered by the states, allocate less of their funds for social services. However, the 15 percent limit was relaxed by Congress in that part of the program in 1990. Plymouth, Massachusetts is using CDBG to develop its long range human services plan.

More details on CDBG and how to access these provisions are available in NLC's *Ways and Means for Children and Families.*

4. Federal-State-Local Administration

More than 40 percent of the federal programs that provide services or resources to children and families in cities and towns are operated by a partnership of the federal and state governments. Most states administer most of these programs through state agencies, but some supervise county administration. Both models will be discussed later, but there are some similarities in the programs, regardless of which administrative model is used. These programs include:

- Aid to Families With Dependent Children (AFDC)
- Medicaid
- Food Stamps
- Social Services Block Grant (SSBG)/ Title XX
- Foster Care
- Child Welfare Services
- Child Care and Development Block Grant (CCDBG)
- School Lunch and Breakfast Programs
- Women, Infants and Children (WIC)
- Education of the Handicapped
- Developmental Disabilities
- Maternal and Child Health Block Grant
- Unemployment Compensation
- Child Support Enforcement

Virtually all of these federal-state programs require a **state plan**, which is prepared by the responsible state agency, signed by the governor, and submitted to the federal government. The state plan outlines exactly how the state is going to spend the program dollars, how the program is organized, and who is responsible for its administration. It also sets state eligibility criteria and benefit levels in those programs that are not uniform throughout the country. For

Services to Vulnerable Children — Child Welfare Services

The most vulnerable children in our society are those who have been physically, emotionally, or sexually abused or neglected. Their families are often suffering multiple problems. The system responsible to care for these children and families, the child welfare system, is perhaps in greater fluctuation right now than any other system. This creates opportunities for you. Many communities have chosen to become involved in family-centered services designed to preserve families and prevent unnecessary out-of-home placement. Some definitions are necessary, if you are to understand these programs well enough to influence what is available to your community's families and children. Some of the current buzz-words can be misleading.

Child Welfare Services: Services that support and promote the well-being of children, and which supplement or support family life, including child protection services, foster care, adoption, child care, child-rearing and homemaking assistance, and counseling.

Child Protective Services: Services designed to protect children from imminent danger of abuse, neglect, exploitation, or abandonment.

Foster Care: Substitute living arrangements for children who have been removed from their homes or abandoned. Includes individual foster families, small group homes, and larger treatment facilities.

Reasonable Efforts: Public Law 96-272 requires that "reasonable efforts" be made to prevent placement before a child is taken from his or her home. Unfortunately, there has been no clear definition of what actions satisfy this requirement. Further, the types of services generally needed by these families are often in short supply or unavailable to them.

Family Preservation Services: Intensive, in-home, family-centered services designed to prevent the unnecessary placement of a child in out-of-home care. These services are usually provided to families in crisis, when removal of a child or children from the home is imminent. They are short-term, flexible, and provided by specifically trained caseworkers, with small case loads, who are available on a 24-hour basis.

Homebuilders: One of the earliest and best-known models of intensive, short-term, family preservation services, started in Tacoma, Washington more than ten years ago. "Families First with Bill Moyers" aired on PBS in March 1992, described similar efforts that have been started in about 25 states.

In-Home Services: Any services provided in the home of the family, rather than in the office of the worker. Often refers to longer-term, less intensive services designed to assist families overcome difficulties that could lead to the break-up of the family.

Family-Based Services: Services that are provided to a family as a unit and seek to build on family strengths.

The optimum service delivery system would include a continuum of all of these service types, but your state's financing mechanisms may need to be changed to make it easier to create such a local system. As you do in all situations, be sure the problem is accurately identified before you seek to solve it. Your community may have more children needing foster care than it has foster families to care for them. But is the real problem a lack of foster families or a lack of family support services that could reduce the need for foster care?

States like Iowa, Illinois, and Michigan are beginning to provide some local flexibility to move Foster Care funds into preventive, family-based services with the intention of strengthening the families so they can stay together and become safe and nurturing. Several national foundations, including the Edna McConnell Clark Foundation (250 Park Avenue, New York, N.Y. 10177-0036) have been active in funding services designed to prevent unnecessary family break-ups. The Clark Foundation published *For Children's Sake: The Promise of Family Preservation* in March 1992, one of the best descriptions of family preservation philosophy and services.

example, each state sets its own benefit levels for AFDC and decides which of the non-mandatory Medicaid services to provide. Most state plans are submitted annually, but the first Child Care and Development Block Grant (CCDBG) plan covered three years, and subsequent CCDBG plans will be required every two years.

The state plan is essentially a contract between the governments involved that governs how the program will be operated. You need to be aware of its importance, and you can provide input to its annual development either through the state agency or governor's office. If you know of a type of program that has had great success in another state, it is important to find out whether your state plan for that particular funding source includes authority to spend the federal money in that way. Local officials with innovative ideas can be influential in pushing state and federal program bureaucracies to allow for those innovations, within the law.

In many of these programs, there is a **matching** requirement for states or localities that wish to participate. Some matching formulas are very complex, like that of the Medicaid program, which ranges from a 50 percent federal share in some states to a maximum federal share of 83 percent. The matching rates for other programs, such as Foster Care and AFDC, are based on the Medicaid rate. The state share of these entitlement programs can be a significant state budget item. As you are probably well aware, federal and state governments will sometimes try to control their costs in a program by changing the matching formula or rate, requiring a greater portion of the cost to be borne by others.

State Administration

Most states (see chart, right) administer the major state-federal programs from the state level through executive branch departments.

How Programs are Administered

S   State administration and delivery
C   County administration
V   Varies among areas within state
M   Mixture of state, county and/or community-based delivery

	Child Welfare	Juvenile Justice	Mental Health
Alabama	C	S	M
Alaska	S	S	M
Arizona	S	S	M
Arkansas	S	S	M
California	C	M	C
Colorado	C	S	M
Connecticut	S	S	S
Delaware	S	S	S
Florida	S	S	M
Georgia	C	M	M
Hawaii	V	S	M
Idaho	S	S	S
Illinois	S	M	S
Indiana	S	M	M
Iowa	S	M	M
Kansas	S	S	S
Kentucky	S	S	M
Louisiana	S	S	M
Maine	S	S	M
Maryland	C	S	C
Massachusetts	S	S	M
Michigan	S	M	M
Minnesota	C	M	C
Mississippi	S	M	M
Missouri	S	M	S
Montana	S	M	M
Nebraska	S	S	M
Nevada	V	M	S
New Hampshire	S	S	M
New Jersey	M	S	M
New Mexico	S	S	M
New York	C	S	M
North Carolina	C	M	M
North Dakota	C	S	C
Ohio	C	S	M
Oklahoma	S	S	M
Oregon	S	S	M
Pennsylvania	M	C	C
Rhode Island	S	S	S
South Carolina	C	S	S
South Dakota	S	S	M
Tennessee	S	S	M
Texas	S	S	S
Utah	S	S	C
Vermont	S	S	M
Virginia	C	V	M
Washington	S	S	C
West Virginia	S	S	M
Wisconsin	C	C	C
Wyoming	C	S	M

Source: Compiled from charts in *Putting the Pieces Together*, National Conference of State Legislatures, Denver, 1990.

Services are either delivered directly by state employees or provided by private agencies under contracts with the state. In either case, state laws and regulations, in addition to the federal laws and regulations, govern the program, which is operated in accordance with the state plan. As discussed in Chapter Two, there is opportunity for your input at each of these steps, but it will probably not be sought out — you will need to decide what is specifically important to your community and take a stand. Some suggestions and examples follow.

The legislature usually includes in the state budget those federal funds that will be administered by the state. The decisions made during the budgeting process can have a major impact on any program's ability to be innovative and respond to the changing needs in your community. This is, naturally, a key point for advocacy for your community needs. You will be most effective if you have a clear and specific vision of what your community needs and why. (See Chapter Five, page 56.)

The budget process is also where your broader advocacy for all children and families of your state can be important.

AFDC: Poverty is the greatest single risk factor for children and families. However, in ten states, the maximum AFDC benefit for a family of three is set at one-third of the poverty line. Over all, benefits range from $120 a month in Mississippi to $891 in Alaska, with only five states providing as much as 75 percent of poverty.[6]

But there is pressure to decrease rather than increase these meager benefits, the primary recipients of which are children. From 1970 to 1991, typical benefits declined by 42 percent, when adjusted for inflation.[7] Increased AFDC benefits will not lift the families of your community out of poverty, but they can certainly improve the ability of families to meet their children's basic needs. For the families of your town, this could be one of your most important advocacy targets. Remember, too, that AFDC benefits are generally spent immediately in the local economy for food, housing, and clothing.

Medicaid: How is your state's Medicaid program responding to the new flexibility provided under the budget acts of 1989 and 1990? This is one place where Congress has provided for state and local innovations. It is up to us to use it well. Georgia, Colorado, and South Carolina are using local health department employees as designated outreach workers for children in need of screening and treatment services, under a Medicaid contract. South Carolina has doubled the number of eligible children receiving the screening they are **entitled** to. Your school nurses might be designated as eligible providers under this program, thus bringing new entitlement dollars into your community, and better health care to the children.

There are many other ways families can benefit from the changes in Medicaid over the last few years. But to take advantage of them, your state must include them in its state plan and provide the matching money. The National Governors' Association published in 1991 a policy report on strategies for improving state child health programs. *Caring For Kids* is a good overview of how states are responding to the new Medicaid flexibility. The Center For the Study of Social Policy also has published *Leveraging Dollars, Leveraging Change, The Use of Medicaid To Support Community-Based Services to Children and Families*, and other detailed working papers on innovative uses of Medicaid and Family Preservation Services, among others. You can order these documents directly from these organizations, whose addresses are in Appendix B.

If you have a good idea for your community, you may be able to convince your state to try it on a pilot basis. For example, "case management services can be targeted to high-risk population groups and substate geographic areas."[8] This means that, unlike most services, which must be provided state-wide, if they are provided at all, case management can be limited to a specific area or population. The states of New York and Washington use this provision to provide case management services to pregnant and parenting teens. If your community wants to assist pregnant teenagers by providing case managers assigned to help them navigate the service system and get the best possible services, you could propose to your state Medicaid agency that the cost of the case managers be covered by Medicaid under this provision.

Tennessee, Michigan, and West Virginia have redefined their Medicaid programs to include some special services to abused or mentally ill children who are in foster care. Oklahoma has amended its state plan to include family preservation services, under certain conditions. Massachusetts has moved to include more services to handicapped children in its Medicaid program.

Effective use of the new Medicaid flexibility can potentially save the state money on improved services to children and families. Perhaps you can interest a local legislator in pursuing it with you. At least you know to ask the question: Can we improve services by taking full advantage of Medicaid options in our state?

Social Services: When Title XX became the Social Services Block Grant (SSBG) in 1981, the requirement for an annual public review of the state plan was dropped. Has your state's SSBG plan been reviewed in the last few years to assure it is still targeting the service areas and population groups of greatest need, and not just the status quo? These questions can and should be asked during the budgeting process. While this state plan no longer must be developed publicly, the state must report annually to the U.S. Department of Health and Human Services on how it spent its allocation in the previous year. Historically, this has been an important funding source for child care and child welfare services in most states.

Child Care: Now that the first three-year plan for the Child Care and Development Block Grant (CCDBG) is in effect, what role will cities play in monitoring its implementation? Under the law, states must consult with local governments in the drafting of the state child care plan, which is also supposed to coordinate with other federal, state, and local child care programs. The state is also required to hold at least one public hearing annually to provide opportunity for public comment. Other possible issues for your policy advocacy on child care are on page 34.

State Supervised, County Administered

Federal law allows the states to choose to administer most programs through local county government. In at least fifteen states, some or all of the major children and family programs are administered by county governments. They are regulated by the federal law, federal regulations, state regulations, and state laws as well. The state is still accountable to the federal government for the development of a state plan and its implementation. But there is often some county flexibility in how resources are deployed. Your advocacy may be particularly effective this close to home, especially if you have a clear community agenda. Usually the counties are required to put up some level of match.

The chart on page 31 shows how certain programs for children and families are administered in the fifty states. Further information about your state's administrative structure for specific programs can be obtained from your state municipal league, or your local legislator's office.

Child Care

According to the 1988-1989 survey done by NLC and published in *Our Future and Our Only Hope,* child care is among the most needed services in cities today. But it is subject to the same kind of fragmentation that affects other intergovernmental services. Even before the new Child Care and Development Block Grant was passed in 1990, a 1988 report by the U.S. General Accounting Office identified forty-six federal programs that provided some type of child care assistance. The same report also found that while federal outlays for child care had increased over the previous decade, those increases were almost exclusively in programs that assist the middle class. Support for low-income families declined as a proportion of the federal child care budget.[*]

The major intergovernmental programs that can help to meet the child care needs of the families in your city include:

- Social Services Block Grant(SSBG)/Title XX
- Child Care and Development Block Grant (CCDBG)
- Community Development Block Grant (CDBG)
- Titles IV-A and IV-E, Child Welfare Services
- AFDC and Family Support Act
- Head Start
- State initiatives for at-risk 4 year olds
- Job Training and Partnership Act
- Family Support Act

Policy issues in implementation of federal-state child care include:

- **Advisory body:**Does your state have a Child Care Advisory Body? Will your state continue the Advisory Body that most states established for the initial implementation of CCDBG? Is local government represented on it?
- **Matching funds:** Is your state taking full advantage of available child care resources by fully matching available federal Title IV-A child care funds?
- **Coordination:** The State Plan for CCDBG could be the vehicle to develop a coordinated system that maximizes resources and expands access to high quality child care for low-income families. If there wasn't time to do that in the first three-year plan, is your state going to use the next two years for this purpose?

- **Consultation with local government:** How is your state complying with the requirement in CCDBG that it must consult with local government?
- **Fees:** Does your state's fee schedule maintain families as they make the transition to economic self-sufficiency or does it provide disincentives to increased earnings?

Issues in developing coordinated local child care programming include:

- **Coordination of eligibility:** Are locally-generated programs carefully targeted to fill gaps in service or do they overlap existing programs? Can your community combine the provision of child care through the federal Family Support Act with the provision of local Head Start to provide full-day care?
- **Getting children ready for kindergarten:** Are all child care and preschool programs aware of the local kindergarten philosophy and curriculum? And are local kindergartens well-versed in the developmental needs of young children?
- **Compensation and staff training:** Are low wages making it difficult to retain trained, experienced child care workers in your programs? The new CCDBG and Head Start monies provide for some salary enhancement and training. How are these funds being used? What training requirements do various programs have? Can joint training be arranged?
- **Cultural competence:** What are the different cultural and ethnic communities in your area? Do your programs actively recruit teachers and administrative staff from those communities? Is training available to assure culturally competent staff?
- **Referral mechanisms:** What happens if a family is turned down by one program? Are they referred to another? If they are eligible for a more comprehensive program, are they referred?
- **JTPA and other JOBS programs:** Is your local Private Industry Council (PIC) using all available child care money for the benefit of working mothers? Are parents encouraged to use high quality child care providers or are incentives built in to use the cheapest possible?

[*] U.S. General Accounting Office. *Child Care: Government Funding Sources, Coordination, and Service Availability,* p. 2, Washington, D.C. 1989.

5. State-Local Programs

Although all levels of government are now involved, to some extent, in most policy areas, traditionally states have been more involved than the federal government in juvenile justice, education, mental health, and child care. Some states have been more active than others, and to some extent, this is what has prompted the federal government's involvement — a desire to assure that residents of all states have access to some level of service. As previously mentioned, even in those programs that are federally-initiated, decisions made at the state level are critical to the effectiveness of the service. It is not possible here to provide even an overview of the myriad of state-generated programs available across the country, and the variety of ways they are provided. When the National Conference of State Legislatures attempted to get a focus on state systems, it found that:

"administrative organizations and service delivery approaches combine to create an over-all 'mega-system' that is both complex and unique to each state. These systems are rooted in a particular political, demographic, social, and even geographical context that includes variables such as state-local relationships, interest groups, the role of the judiciary, public-private interaction, and distribution of the population."[9]

What this tells every locally elected advocate is that there are many ways to approach any problem, and the one your state has chosen may have worked once, but could be open to review and change any time. In other words, never take "No, we can't afford it," or "No, we never did it that way before," for answers. Always ask "Is there another way we could define this problem?" "Has someone else devised a solution we could use as a model?" "Are there other resources we could use, if we were a little more creative?"

In 1990, the Children's Defense Fund (CDF) measured trends in children's well-being in every state on the basis of ten indicators over the last decade. CDF also measured each state's investment in improving children's lives. The states were then ranked and the results were published in *Children 1990*. This book, which is available from CDF (122 C Street NW, Washington, D.C. 20001), gives you an idea of how your state fared when reviewed against all the other states by national advocates. Alabama, New Hampshire, and Vermont ranked highest, while Arizona and Maryland ranked lowest. These rankings can give you an idea of where your state is considered weak, and they may point out some areas where you will want to focus advocacy efforts.

The KIDS COUNT Data Book also provides state-by-state information on nine indicators of child well-being. The 1992 edition ranks North Dakota first overall and Mississippi last. The KIDS COUNT Data Book is published by the Center for the Study of Social Policy (Suite 503, 1250 Eye Street NW, Washington, D.C. 20005) with funding from the Annie E. Casey Foundation.

State-wide child and family advocacy groups exist in many states, and they are another resource to tap. (See Appendix A for a list.) In addition to their knowledge of state-level programming, policy, and legislative issues, many are also involved with local issues and local implementation of state programs.

6. Locally Generated Programs

The traditional programs of cities and counties, including recreation and police, create the environment within which all of the other programs and services are provided. For example, a strong after-school recreation program and a police commitment to community and crime prevention will have a major impact on all services. It is important that the local infrastructure supports children and families in ways that can make the other kinds of services more effective. Your questions during city budget hearings or when new programs are brought to the City Council for approval can be critical. Ask about connections with other services and programs. If it is a crisis-intervention program, ask about prevention. If public housing wants to build new units, ask about the social services to support the families who will live in those units. Ask questions about city support for nonsocial service aspects of the needs of families, such as those met by community-based organizations and economic development activities.

The Consortium of Family Organizations (COFO) has developed a checklist of questions you can ask to determine the impact on families of any new or existing program or policy. (See page 37.) You can use these questions informally as you review and develop programs, or they could be the basis of a required "Family Impact Review" for all proposals that come before your city council.

In Florida, the legislature has given the residents of each county the authority to vote to increase property taxes and dedicate the proceeds to youth services. In Pinellas County (St. Petersburg), the Juvenile Welfare Board has been funded in this way since 1945. Jim Mills, Executive Director of this autonomous local body, finds that the biggest advantage to the locally generated dollars is that they are totally discretionary and can be used for preventive and "glue" services (that is, services that hold the pieces together) even when other governments are cutting in those areas. Having local control over discretionary funds allows the people who really know the neighborhoods and community to make the decisions. "Common sense and wisdom do not grow proportionately as you approach the state capitol", he says. But he cautions that it takes constant leadership and monitoring to assure that local funds do not supplant other funds or provide incentives to the state to reduce its share. This same caution has been voiced by people in cities such as Minneapolis and Seattle where local voters have approved dedicated taxes for children and family services.

In moving to provide better services, you must be sure that the local program issues have been correctly identified. You may be convinced that you have a shortage of preschool child care in your community, but before you begin pushing for more state or federal aid, be sure that your own policies are not discouraging the development of more programs.

One community found that its zoning code required half again as much outside space per child as the state licensing regulations. While this may have been appropriate when it was a land-rich suburb, the realities of land prices and lot sizes had changed so that it was no longer economically feasible for new programs to meet these standards. The child care advocates in the community believed the state standards to be sufficient for optimal child development, and cooperated in amending the zoning code to comply with them. This opened the door for several new child care centers and changed the intergovernmental issue the city needed to address from availability to affordability. They now had enough child care spaces, but their low-income working families needed subsidies in order to use them.

Checklist: A Tool for Analysis

Check those principles and questions that apply to the particular program or policy.

1. **Family support and responsibilities:** Policies and programs should aim to support and supplement family functioning and provide substitute services only as a last resort.

   ☐ How does the proposal (or existing program) support and supplement parents' and other family members' ability to carry out their responsibilities?

   ☐ Does it provide incentives for other persons to take over family functioning when doing so may not be necessary?

   ☐ What effects does it have on marital commitment or parental obligations?

   ☐ What effects does it have on adult children's ties to their elderly parents?

2. **Family membership and stability:** Whenever possible, policies and programs should encourage and reinforce marital, parental, and family commitment and stability, especially when children are involved. Intervention in family membership and living arrangements is usually justified only to protect family members from serious harm or at the request of the family itself.

   ☐ What incentives or disincentives does the policy or program provide to marry, separate, or divorce?

   ☐ What incentives or disincentives are provided to give birth to, foster, or adopt children?

   ☐ What criteria are used to justify removal of a child or adult from the family?

   ☐ What resources are allocated to help keep the family together when this is the appropriate goal?

   ☐ What services are provided to help family members living apart remain connected and, if appropriate, come together again?

3. **Family involvement and interdependence:** Policies and programs must recognize the interdependence of family relationships, the strength and persistence of family ties and obligations, and the wealth of resources that families can mobilize to help their members.

   ☐ To what extent does the policy or program design recognize the influence of the family context upon the individual's need or problem?

   ☐ To what extent does it involve immediate and extended family members in working toward a solution?

   ☐ To what extent does it acknowledge the power and persistence of family ties, especially when they are problematic or destructive?

   ☐ How does it assess and balance the competing needs, rights, and interests of various members of a family?

4. Family partnership and empowerment: Policies and programs must encourage individuals and their close family members to collaborate as partners with program professionals in the delivery of services to an individual. In addition, parent and family representatives are an essential resource in policy development, program planning, and evaluation.

☐ In what specific ways does the proposed or existing program provide full information and a range of choices to individuals and their close family members?

☐ In what ways is the policy/program sensitive to the complex realities of families' lives and their need to manage and coordinate the multiple services they often require?

☐ In what ways do program professionals work in collaboration with the families of their clients, patients, or students?

☐ In what ways does the program or policy involve parents and family representatives in policy and program development, implementation, and evaluation?

5. Family diversity: Families come in many forms and configurations, and policies and programs must take into account their different effects on different types of families. Policies and programs must acknowledge and value the diversity of family life and not discriminate against or penalize families solely for reasons of structure, roles, cultural values, or life stage.

☐ How does the proposal or program affect various types of families?

☐ If the proposed or existing program targets only certain families, for example, only employed parents or single parents, what is the justification? Does it discriminate against or penalize other types of families for insufficient reason?

☐ How does it identify and respect the different values, attitudes, and behaviors of families from various racial, ethnic, religious, and cultural backgrounds that are relevant to program effectiveness?

6. Targeting vulnerable families: Families in greatest economic and social need, as well as those determined to be most vulnerable to breakdown, should have first priority in government policies and programs.

☐ Does the proposed or existing program identify and target publicly supported services for families in the most extreme economic or social need?

☐ Does it give priority and preventive services to families who are most vulnerable to breakdown?

*Taken from the Consortium of Family Organizations (COFO) *Family Policy Report,* Vol. 1, No. 1. March 1990, which was adapted from *A Strategy for Strengthening Families: Using Family Criteria in Policymaking and Program Evaluation.* Edited by Theodora Ooms and Steven Preister. A consensus report of the Family Criteria Task Force. Washington, D.C.: Family Impact Seminar, 1988. Reprinted with permission.

7. School Districts and Municipal Government

The type of intergovernmental interaction most often reported in the NLC questionnaires was that between cities and schools. In some areas, city government has some jurisdiction over the budget or governance of the schools. But, in most cities the two are separately elected functions. For example, in Cambridge, Massachusetts, the mayor is also head of the school committee — a one-person collaboration. Cambridge city councillor Alice Wolf, who recently completed her term as mayor and also completed her term as co-chair of NLC's Task Force on Cities' Roles in Education, identifies four important ingredients for developing partnerships between cities and schools:

"1. Focus on the existing conditions in the community that make it ripe for a partnership effort.

2. Look at how to utilize existing responsibilities and relationships.

3. Assess the formal governance structure that does or does not bind the local government and schools.

4. Develop the political leadership that puts children on the front burner."[10]

The kinds of programs offered jointly by cities and school districts vary widely. Many cities have developed joint purchasing agreements for items that both entities use in volume and that are cheaper when purchased in bulk. Thornton, Colorado, was urged by its residents to create more cross-jurisdictional use of school and city facilities, resulting in more available space for its citizens and better citizen support.

At the other end of the spectrum, schools in some areas are becoming the sites for local delivery of many social services. New Beginnings in San Diego is an example of a community coming together to improve educational and social outcomes for children by assessing their needs and providing co-located and coordinated services based at the school.

A 1991 publication by the National School Boards Association (NSBA), *Link-up: A Resource Directory*, describes 171 interagency collaborations to help children (NSBA, 1680 Duke Street, Alexandria, Va. 22314).

Notes

1. Select Committee on Children, Youth and Families. *Federal Programs Affecting Children and Their Families, 1990*, p.8, U.S.House of Representatives, Washington, D.C. 1990.
2. Children's Defense Fund. *An Opinion Maker's Guide to Children in Election Year 1992*, Washington, D.C. 1991.
3. National Commission on Child Welfare and Family Preservation. *Factbook on Public Child Welfare Services and Staff*, p. 3, American Public Welfare Association, Washington, D.C. 1990.
4. Select Committee on Children, Youth and Families. *Federal Programs Affecting Children and Their Families, 1990*, p. 39, U.S. House of Representatives, Washington, D.C. 1990.
5. Children's Defense Fund. *Children 1990: A Report Card, Briefing Book, and Action Primer*, p. 96, Washington, D.C. 1990.
6. Children's Defense Fund. *An Opinion Maker's Guide to Children in Election Year 1992*, p. 73, Washington, D.C. 1991.
7. Center on Budget and Policy Priorities. *The States and the Poor*, p. 8, Washington, D.C. 1991.

8. The Center For The Study of Social Policy. *The Use of Medicaid To Support Community-Based Services To Children And Families,* p. 15, Washington, D.C. 1988.

9. Robison, Susan. *Putting The Pieces Together,* p. ix, National Conference of State Legislatures, Denver, 1990.

10. Wolf, Alice. Speech to National Civic League, November 17, 1990; reprinted in *Nation's Cities Weekly,* December 12, 1990, National League of Cities, Washington, D.C.

CHAPTER FOUR

Local Government: Catalyst for Collaboration

How do you eat an elephant? One bite at a time."
  —Bishop Desmond Tutu

"If you are standing at the edge of a chasm, you don't try to get over it one step at a time, you take a leap."
  —Author Lisbeth Schorr

Having reviewed the various ways intergovernmental programs for children and families are provided in this country, the rational observer might conclude that it is too complex to make sense of and resolve to advocate an entire overhaul of the federal system. There have been some attempts to do this, under the name of services integration, which will be briefly noted in this chapter. There are at least two other approaches that may be more within reach, and they are suggested in the two quotations at the beginning of this chapter. As you ponder the maze or array of services available and the needs in your community, do you feel like you are ready for a "leap" or a "bite"?

If you, like Lisbeth Schorr, are ready to take a major leap, you can take the leadership in developing a comprehensive, intergovernmental, collaborative effort in your local community. You do not have to fix all the problems of all the systems — instead you can create a mechanism that will work to rationalize service delivery to the needs of the children and families in your city or town. Some examples of this course of action will be discussed in this chapter along with the shift toward these local initiatives in the entire service integration field.

You may, however, feel more in common with Bishop Tutu as he tried to change the system of government in South Africa. Your community may not be ready to take a leap, and a more incremental approach may be preferable. Chapter Five will help you to position yourself and your community to take advantage of every possible resource in the most effective manner possible, and to take bigger and bigger bites out of the elephant that is children's services.

Service Integration

For more than twenty years, people have been talking about (and some have been trying) the integration of human service delivery systems into a cohesive whole that would have the flexibility to treat families as a unit and people as whole beings — not just accumulations of problems, each of which must be dealt with separately. Cities and towns, whose budgets are often stretched by the multiple-needs clients most affected by fragmentation, have always had a stake in this movement. Over the years, though, most of these efforts have been "top down", because most of the systems problems are generated at the highest levels — often in the laws themselves. It was thought that the problems had to be attacked at their perceived source.

Many observers believe they are now witnessing a paradigm shift in the unfolding events in services for children and families, nationally. Conventional wisdom now seems to contend that real change in the way people are treated in a system is more likely to come at that point in the system that is closest to the people. Systems don't serve people — people do. The failures of the current nonsystems to facilitate people helping people are most obvious at the delivery level. To local community leaders, the problems of program fragmentation have real faces; there are real families who are falling through the cracks. Local motivation and innovation can be sparked by the local results of systems failures. Although, as Mayor Frances Huntley-Cooper of Fitchburg, Wisconsin, says, "It is too bad a system has to fail and hit close to home before society wakes up ...."[1]

It is important to keep a realistic perspective as you consider these issues. Services integration and collaboration will not create resources. This is not a solution to the chronic underfunding of many services for children. Your advocacy is needed to improve the level of fiscal commitment to children and families at all levels of government. Michael Kirst, who heads Policy Analysis for California Education (PACE) at Stanford University, concluded after three years of research that "tenacious collaboration alone will not make up for our societal underinvestment in children." But, he adds, "the system as a whole is so fundamentally flawed that huge amounts of dollars dumped in wouldn't do much good."[2]

Sid Gardner states that "we are ultimately failing our children not only because we haven't invested in them, but also because as communities we have failed to work together to hold ourselves accountable for the substantial resources we do invest — and for the outcomes of our most vulnerable residents."[3]

A brief history of intergovernmental attempts to develop integrated service delivery systems, titled *Services Integration: A Twenty-Year Retrospective*, has been published by the Office of the Inspector General in the U.S.

Department of Health and Human Services (HHS). While the report concludes that service integration attempts "have been instrumental in making human services more accessible to clients and more responsive to their needs", it goes on to find that "over the long term," these efforts "have had little institutional impact on a highly fragmented human services system."[4]

A companion report, also done by the Office of the Inspector General, *Services Integration for Families and Children in Crisis*, identifies and analyzes several "efforts initiated at the community level to assist dysfunctional or multiproblem children and families." These and other analyses have spurred a new federal interest in services integration. Martin Gerry, the Assistant Secretary for Planning and Evaluation at HHS, is spearheading a new federal effort to encourage state and local initiatives. As a part of this effort, HHS has awarded several grants to stimulate the development of resources and technical assistance for communities. Details on some of these are described at the end of this chapter.

This shift in emphasis to the local level is accompanied by another major difference between the service integration movement of the 1970s and current efforts. While the education community was not actively involved in earlier years, schools are now major players in most local collaboration initiatives. Having come face-to-face with the reality that you can't educate children who are hungry or homeless, some educators and school districts are leading their local communities into more family-centered thinking and programming. National organizations, such as the National School Boards Association, the Council of Chief State School Officers, and the Education Commission of the States, are also taking prominent roles in this area.

An example is Kentucky's Education Reform Act of 1990. In addition to making major changes in the education system, the Act has made it the responsibility of local schools to assure that all families eligible for the free lunch program also receive needed support services. State and federal funds are made available to the schools to develop family service centers (on or near the school site) designed to build the family and community support that will enable a child to succeed in school. The centers are required to involve and empower parents and to aggressively coordinate existing community resources.

As you prepare to take your leap into collaborative services, keep in mind that integration is not an end in itself. It is the means to make services fit the people they serve. Those services must be developed with a clear understanding of the great diversity of family life in today's society, and they must seek to treat children and families with respect for their individual dynamics, cultures, strengths, and weaknesses.

You will need a mechanism that is capable of functioning in at least three basic roles:

1. A neutral and authoritative convenor of all service providers.

2. A change agent, able to provide incentives for collaboration with local discretionary resources.

3. An evaluator that uses child and family centered outcome measures to force programs to fit together to meet their real needs.

At the same time, it is important to:

■ Think families, not programs.
■ Think community, not jurisdiction.
■ Stay focused on your goal to strengthen and nurture families and children, not programs or organizations.

To help you choose the best approach for your community, this chapter will highlight several current examples of multi-disciplinary local intergovernmental collaborations that are focused on restructuring or improving systems and services. There are several other communities that could also have been on this short list, but these four give a diverse picture of the various kinds of efforts going on right now. You are welcome to contact any of the cities mentioned for more detail.

Minneapolis Youth Coordinating Board
Minneapolis, Minn. (population 370,951)

Former Representative Don Fraser became mayor of Minneapolis in 1980. He was already well aware of the fragmentation of state and federal child and family programs, and he quickly realized that the local situation was equally problematic. As mayor of the largest city in Hennepin County, he represented only one of several elected bodies with some jurisdiction over programs for children. There were the separately elected Board of Education, Minneapolis Park and Recreation Board, Minneapolis Public Library Board, and the Hennepin County Board of Commissioners. During the early 1980s, he began meeting with other elected officials to explore how collaborative efforts could improve conditions for children. They soon found that the type of joint powers agreement they would need in order to act together on any of their shared problems was not authorized by state law. So the first step was

A Mayor's View

Mayor Don Fraser of Minneapolis talks about his evolving views on local services for children and families.

"Over the years, my thinking has changed about the most appropriate kinds of services our city should be offering for children and families. I have been through three phases.

At first, when I looked at the needs of children, I saw the bad outcomes, such as teen pregnancy and high school dropouts, and felt that targeted intervention to those children most at risk was the best programming strategy. After a while, I came to the conclusion that dealing with the children after the fact — after their lives had already become problematic — could not turn things around for the community.

At that point, we moved to get involved earlier in the lives of our children, in the belief that if we worked with them from conception, supporting the family as a nurturing environment, we could have more impact. We supported early childhood development programs, and our Youth Coordinating Board developed the neighborhood-based, home visitation prevention and school-readiness program, Way-To-Grow.

Both of these strategies are valuable and viable, but I have now come to see that neither targeted intervention nor preventive strategies that begin with early childhood will work very well unless we also address the need for stronger communities that encourage the *connections* and *relationships* necessary to create informal support networks for families. People need to be connected to their neighborhood in order to become part of the community. Out of this can come the support which is generated by the resulting relationships.

When we looked at our neighborhoods carefully, we found that poor families move a lot, which is very disruptive to kids. In trying to understand why, we found that, for a variety of reasons, roots were missing for these families — they didn't know their neighbors and did not feel connected to the community. The neighborhoods they lived in didn't encourage or adequately support the making of useful connections. For example, parks can be important to a community, both in offering recreation and in creating opportunities for socialization.

to take a very pro-active position and get the legislature to provide such authority.

While Fraser does not believe that such joint meetings and collaboration must necessarily be formalized, it was important for Minneapolis to have a formal structure in order to assure that each jurisdiction could put money into the coordinating board to fund a budget adequate to support a small staff.

The Minneapolis Youth Coordinating Board was established in 1985 "to ensure the healthy growth and development of the nearly 88,500 children (ages 0 to 20) in Minneapolis." The eleven-member board was created jointly by the city, Minneapolis Public Schools, Hennepin County, the Minneapolis Park and Recreation Board, and the Minneapolis Public

Library Board. It also includes a member of the state senate and house of representatives, and a juvenile court judge. There is a strong commitment to involvement on the part of the elected officials, personally. The staff does the follow-up work, but Mayor Fraser and the other elected members take the leadership on policy matters.

One of the first actions of the Board was to develop "City's Children 2007", a twenty-year vision and set of goals for the City, which serves as the basic policy document for the rest of the Board's work and also helps to guide individual policy decisions on the part of the various member organizations.

The Coordinating Board does not provide direct services, but it has been instrumental in the development of several programs for

"When we held neighborhood meetings to find out what was on people's minds, the surprising and unanimous call was for safer parks with longer hours and more organized programs. The chief complaint was that the parks were not open on evenings and weekends. Under-used parks represent a loss of a valuable community resource which can help to create a neighborhood sense of togetherness.

I have often been asked why the city should be involved in children's issues. The first answer was that we needed to get involved because children were not getting the support they need. But now we are beginning to understand the importance of community. To the extent that a robust community plays (or can play) an important role in assisting families with young children, the city's role becomes ever clearer. It is squarely a municipal job to help weave the community fabric that can strengthen families and neighborhoods. Mayors and city councils must look at their neighborhoods and traditional services through new eyes. Parks, schools, and neighborhood organizations help create connections. So do festivals in the parks and social activities by block clubs. A community that supports and encourages scouting may be reducing its future dropout rate by giving kids more self-worth and a feeling of belonging.

When our school district planned a referendum for school funding this year, we urged them to include money for preschool and school-readiness activities. They agreed and set aside $3 million of the total $25 million package. Even though only 17 percent of our families have children, the referendum passed by a 2-to-1 margin.

This $3 million will get us started on a series of neighborhood school-readiness centers, to include day care, Head Start, kindergarten, Way-To-Grow, and other family support activities. The city council has begun to help find funding for buildings. We will draw on every possible source of support to create neighborhood-based centers in which parents and children feel welcome and can become more connected to one another and to their community and begin to form the kinds of relationships that will stabilize and strengthen family life."

(Interviewed by the author, September 1991)

20-Year Vision of the Ideal Minneapolis Community

In the year 2007, the ideal Minneapolis community...

I. ...is one in which the basic needs of every person are met in order to permit each child to fully benefit from developmental opportunities.

II. ...promotes the full development of every child in the areas of physical, social, emotional, cognitive and moral/spiritual growth.

III. ...recognizes, practices and teaches evolving community values that reflect both the diversity and the shared destiny of the community.

IV. ...demonstrates a collective commitment to the raising and development of children.

V. ...has economic, environmental and political systems that promote the health, development and well-being of children.

Source: Minneapolis Youth Coordinating Board

youth-at-risk, and has obtained foundation funding to assist with its research and coordination functions. A foundation-funded study developed the "Way-To-Grow" program of home health visitors who focus on school readiness by age 5. The Board then lobbied the state legislature for continuing money for the program.

Fraser is candid about the fact that it has been difficult for the state to become a collaborative partner in Minneapolis' efforts. "The state is handicapped by turf and categorical thinking. Collaboration is usually thought of as a new program or an add-on, but it is best when it can be seen as part of the job of an agency. Lack of ownership on the part of an agency can be fatal to good collaboration."

Mayor Fraser also suggests that local officials become thoroughly familiar with both the bureaucratic structure of the executive branch agencies and the legislative process. "If you feel at home with the process, it is easier to influence it. It also becomes easier to understand the perspective of the people with whom you are dealing, if you understand the processes within which they are working."

Richard Mammen, the Executive Director of the Youth Coordinating Board, can be contacted at 202 City Hall, Minneapolis, MN 55415 or (612) 348-6995.

New Futures for Little Rock Youth
Little Rock, Ark., (population 158,915)

New Futures For Little Rock Youth is a nonprofit agency, created in 1988, specifically to be the lead agency in carrying out the New Futures project goals. "A total of twenty-three diverse agencies and organizations representing both state and local government, private business and non-profit agencies have banded together to pool their time, energy and resources toward alleviating at-risk youth problems." The five-year goals of the organization include: "decreasing teen pregnancies and births, decreasing youth inactivity and unemployment, improving graduation rates and attendance rates in grades seven to twelve. Finally, New Futures seeks to promote public awareness of the problems of at-risk youth in general."[5]

The local money that matched the Annie E. Casey Foundation's (see note, next page) challenge grant included sizable investments from the City of Little Rock, the Arkansas Department of Human Services, the Arkansas Department of Health, the Little Rock School District, the Arkansas business community, and other sources, including non-profit organizations.

The original leadership in developing New Futures for Little Rock Youth came jointly from the city manager and the superintendent of schools. Both kept their elected officials well-informed and received support from them. This has been important, because momentum was somewhat dulled by turnover in the superintendent's position, a situation that has now stabilized. Over time, the personal involvement of these elected officials becomes even more critical, as the project moves into controversial issues, like school restructuring.

Tom Dalton, Little Rock's city manager and current chair of New Futures For Little Rock Youth, has been involved from the beginning. He believes that the collaborative process is becoming well-enough institutionalized in Little Rock that it will continue beyond the Casey Foundation grant period. It has not been an easy process to change the way people make decisions. He cautions that it is very important for people to gain

> "a clear understanding of how a collaborative differs from a classic board. Consensus is important and diverse views must be accommodated, but if each member doesn't feel bound by the decisions made by the collaborative, it falls apart. That means shared decision

making, and that's a big hurdle for some. I have to do more than simply sit in meetings and carry back information — I have to be willing to change the way I do things based on what happened in the meeting. Public policy reached by this process is more enduring."[6]

According to Dalton, one of the benefits of the project to date is the "amazing amounts of data" it has amassed. These data, taken together with anecdotal reports from the case managers, are providing decision and policy makers with information they have not had access to before. This information is useful both in showing where progress is being made and where problems have different dimensions. One case summary, prepared for the collaborative by one of the case managers, showed the difficulties faced by a thirteen-year-old girl, her incarcerated mother, and the extended family members who were trying to care for her. In all, 14 agencies were involved with the family, but no one had yet been able to make the systems "work" for the benefit of this child. Having a case manager in place does not automatically cause the systems to come together. But it does give

---

* The mission of the Annie E. Casey Foundation is "strengthening systems and environments to improve life outcomes for disadvantaged children." The Foundation believes that its greatest potential for improving the well-being of kids ultimately lies in its ability to influence the major institutions that serve disadvantaged children and the public-policy environment that shapes how those institutions define and deal with the needs of children and families. "Accordingly, the Foundation looks for opportunities to make strategic investments to change the policies and practices of key institutions and whole communities and to demonstrate how these changes can lead to improved outcomes for disadvantaged children." (AECF June, 1991)

The New Futures Initiative, which began in 1987, was designed to reduce school dropouts and school failure, teen pregnancy, and youth unemployment. The Foundation, however, recognized that these issues were really symptoms of underlying dilemmas regarding the ways that communities and systems viewed and worked with youth. To address both the goals and the underlying dilemmas, and after an extensive search process, the Foundation awarded five-year grants to five cities that currently include: Dayton, Ohio; Little Rock, Arkansas; Pittsburgh, Pennsylvania; and Savannah, Georgia. Each city was challenged to develop and implement four basic components: an oversight collaborative; a case management system; integrated services for youth; and a management information system.

Each of these communities was required to put up matching funding, and each has developed in its own unique fashion. We will highlight two of these efforts. More information can be obtained by contacting Bonnie Politz of the Annie E. Casey Foundation at One Lafayette Place, Greenwich, Connecticut 06830 or (203) 661-2773.

---

the collaborative the opportunity to address the very real issues caused by the fragmentation.

Don Crary, the executive director of New

"A common theme borrowed from African folklore runs through our community: 'It takes a whole village to raise a child'."
—Lottie Shackelford, City Director, Little Rock.

Futures for Little Rock Youth, can be contacted at 209 W. Capitol Avenue, Second Floor Annex, Little Rock, AR 72201 or (501) 374-1011.

Chatham-Savannah Youth Futures Authority
Savannah, Ga., (population 141,654)

According to its Second Phase Plan, the Chatham-Savannah Youth Futures Authority (YFA) is "a group of people who believe the most productive way to help youth is to build an integrated service system that is not constrained by the artificial boundaries of traditional categorical programs."[7]

Created in response to the Annie E. Casey Foundation's challenge, and building upon already existing local initiatives, the YFA includes city, county and state government officials, representatives from the school district (including school board and superintendent) and Savannah State College, local business and civic leaders, as well as human service agencies. The YFA's stated philosophy is that improvement in outcomes for youth "will require fixing systems, not fixing kids: youth should not be blamed for conditions which lead to failure rather than success." Their mission is "To encourage change in the policies, procedures and funding patterns of community institutions needed to enable the youth of our community

to become productive, competent and self-fulfilling adults."[8]

Where they exist, local collaborative governing bodies are often incorporated as non-profit corporations. The YFA is different in two very important ways: it was established by state statute, so it has some intergovernmental clout; and it was empowered by the Legislature to pool funds from multiple sources and jurisdictions, which gives it greater flexibility in breaking down categorical boundaries and fragmentation.

Over its first three years of operation, YFA has developed an impressive list of program initiatives aimed mainly at the goals of reducing teen pregnancy, unemployment, and school dropouts. These range from tutoring and transportation programs, to an ambitious Savannah Compact between the Chamber of Commerce and school system that has the dual goal of improving educational achievement and job readiness, and assuring graduates secure and satisfying work in Savannah.

Of greatest interest, perhaps, are the things the YFA has decided to change in the second phase of the initiative. While most of the efforts during the first phase "were in the form of remedial and add-on programs targeted to middle and high school youth," the second phase approach will include "the creation of a continuum of services designed to prevent youth from becoming at-risk at an early age." Specifically, the YFA decided to broaden its "range of concern from middle and high school students to prenatal through age 18."[9] As one staff member put it: "It felt like we were just a bandaid factory, because we were starting too late. We know the issues that cause a teenager problems began long before — probably before birth. We need to break that cycle."

Rather than expanding its first phase remedial programs to become city-wide as originally planned, the YFA decided to continue existing programs and to use expansion resources to fund several new initiatives outlined in the Second Phase Plan and consistent with its two strategic goals, which are:

> "1. To develop a coordinated system of service to children based on a continuum of care; and
>
> 2. To facilitate and support the restructuring of the educational system to ensure that all children succeed in school."[10]

The new initiatives include:

- Neighborhood-based Service Centers targeting specific neighborhoods and offering a continuum of services, including school readiness programs.
- A Family Case Management System for teenage parents and their infants.
- A Leadership Development Academy to coordinate and provide interinstitutional training for agency personnel and other service providers. Inter-disciplinary training is needed to increase the ability of workers to take a holistic view of the child and his or her situation and needs.
- Intensified work with the school system to review curriculum and policies and to make recommendations for improvement.
- Consideration of a highly specialized curriculum for at-risk black males in the third, sixth, and ninth grades.

The YFA also asked the legislature to expand the membership to allow for the inclusion of more community-based private sector service providers, advocates, and parents.

As the Youth Futures Authority began work on its first strategic goal and the development of Neighborhood Service Centers, it identified several "barriers to services" that will need to be overcome. One of the most interesting intergovernmental challenges facing the group will be its attempt to attack the barriers caused by the plethora of eligibility forms and application procedures that face any person who attempts to receive service from more than one agency or program. A task force has set a target date of 1992 for implementation of common intake and eligibility forms for all of the services that families can access through the Neighborhood Service Centers. This is a complicated task that is made feasible by the fact that the YFA Board includes policy makers from most of the affected systems and levels of government.

YFA's work is also enhanced by the city government's commitment to empowering neighborhood residents to create their own vision for the kind of place they want their neighborhood to be, and to become partners in making that vision a reality.

Otis Johnson, Executive Director of YFA, summarizes his experiences to date in this way:

> "We have learned in Savannah what other governmental officials must remember. True intergovernmental and community collaboration is possible when people from the neighborhoods, and public and private institutions enter a true partnership motivated by a shared vision. Our vision is that every child will grow up to be healthy, be secure, and become literate and economically productive. We all started from different points in understanding the problems of children and families and what needed to be done. However, with this unifying vision, no one disagrees with what we are trying to accomplish."[11]

Dr. Johnson can be contacted at P.O. Box 10212, Savannah, GA 31421 or (912) 651-6810.

Seattle, Wash., (population 493,846)

Children and families in Seattle have been blessed by the presence of strong political leadership. Charles Royer, mayor from 1978 to 1990, and Norman Rice, his successor, both used the power of the office to galvanize community support for improving conditions for Seattle's children and families. They have not used a formal, intergovernmental structure or created a new governing body. Instead, they have taken the position that it is the city's responsibility to provide leadership, planning, and staff support. They have made children and families a top priority for every city department, and enlisted local business, civic groups, and the community in the process.

Through the 1970s and early 1980s, Seattle was faced with a steady out-migration of young families and children. Recognizing that reversing this trend was essential to the city's future economic health, Mayor Royer joined forces with leaders in the business and non-profit sectors to create a family- and child-friendly atmosphere in the city. Seattle KidsPlace was born and began to move children and families higher on the political, economic, and cultural agendas of the city. A detailed survey of children and youth was taken, and The KidsPlace Action Agenda 1985-1990 was developed by more than three hundred volunteers. It generated such activities as KidsDays, when the city's attractions and transportation systems were free to people under sixteen, and KidFriendly logos for businesses that could assist children needing neighborly help.

Mayor Royer required every city department to suggest children's initiatives in their annual budget submissions, and a detailed "Status Report on the City's Children and Youth and the System That Serves Them" was prepared by the city staff. Eventually, KidsPlace became formalized as a non-profit entity in its own right and has continued to support Kid-Friendly activities in the city. In the meantime, the city developed a Youth Policy Plan to institutionalize the emphasis on children and families in all city activities.

When Norman Rice was elected mayor in 1989, he was eager to continue the progress that had been made and to more fully involve the schools.

"To my mind, one of the most promising areas for addressing the needs of our children and families is by creating partnerships between our schools and the more traditional functions of local municipal governments. Increasingly, our teachers are being asked to play counselor, social worker, even police officer. There isn't much room left for teaching.

"But if local government can reclaim some of those traditional roles, in partnership with our schools, then it will allow our teachers and our school to go back to their real mission — giving our children the knowledge and the skills they need to succeed in the 21st Century.

"And when I look at all the potential for local government to get involved in our schools, the possibilities are virtually endless."[12]

One of his first actions was to begin plans for a city-wide Education Summit, which involved more than two thousand Seattle residents in setting common goals for improving the quality of the schools and the educational system. Work groups of teachers, parents, elected officials, and business and labor leaders then took the broad goals and developed 150 concrete program proposals for better schools. The level of community support was so great, that within a very short time, the group had identified more than $1 million in new resources to begin implementation.

One of the major community goals was "to make every child safe, healthy and ready to learn; to secure the child's physical needs and external environment, so that he or she could learn more effectively inside the classroom." To address this need, they put together the Families and Education Levy, a major human services ballot measure, which passed by a 57 percent vote in November, 1990, and provides approximately $8.5 million per year.

By January of 1991, "A Family Support and Development Agenda For the City of Seattle" had been drafted by a Family Support Team of staff from all the affected city departments. A new City Office for Education now has as its mission to build and maintain effective City programs and partnerships with the schools.

William H. ("Woody") Hodge was hired to become Director of the Office of Education and is now involved in joint planning and coordination on a number of fronts. Health services are a county function in Washington, so implementation of the health components of the plan necessitated collaboration with the county. At one working session, he says, "it was like a light bulb went on and we realized we should be doing a lot more joint planning for children and families. We are hoping that that was the beginning of a more regional approach to a health and human services strategy." The county, city, and schools have begun to look at the possibilities of pooling resources, using common sites and looking collaboratively at the needs of all residents in the area, without creating redundant services or systems.

Hodge cautions that it takes time to develop the kind of relationships that allow for collaborative planning. "Don't start off with the assumption that everyone is open-minded and eager for change. Even some people who think they are, find out that they themselves carry

Seven Key Points for Collaboration

Thinking Collaboratively concludes with the following seven key points for policy makers to remember:

1. Collaboration is not a quick fix for many of the vexing problems society faces.

2. Collaboration is a means to an end, not an end in itself.

3. Developing interagency collaboration is extremely time-consuming and process-intensive.

4. Interagency collaboration does not guarantee the development of a client-centered service system nor the establishment of a trusting relationship between an at-risk child or family and a helping adult.

5. Collaboration occurs among people — not among institutions. Workers must be supported at each level of organization where collaboration in expected to take place.

6. Creative problem-solving skills must be developed and nurtured in those expected to collaborate. Among these skills are the ability to deal with the ambiguity and stress that increased discretion brings.

7. Collaboration is too important a concept to be trivialized. It must represent more than the shifting of boxes on an agency organizational chart.

some resistance. Training is needed for managers at all levels to deal with paradigm shifts and change."[13]

Woody Hodge, Director, Office of Education, can be contacted at the Seattle Department of Human Services, 618 Second Avenue, 6th Floor, Seattle, WA 98104-2232, or at (206) 233-5118.

Resources and Technical Assistance

There are sources of information and technical assistance you can tap as you work to improve government services for children and families. Here are some you should know about.

■ Two of the best published resources for anyone interested in developing a more integrated community-based approach for children's services were published in 1991 by the Education and Human Services Consortium in Washington, D.C. The consortium, of which NLC is a member, is a loosely knit coalition of professional membership organizations, advocacy groups, and social policy and research centers. These diverse groups are united by their shared commitment to the creation of an effective and responsive system of education and human services for children and families. *Thinking Collaboratively: Ten Questions and Answers to Help Policy Makers Improve Children's Services* and *What It Takes: Structuring Interagency Partnerships to Connect Children and Families With Comprehensive Services* gather what has been learned in various experiments around the country and provide a clear framework for action and thoughtful review of the issues. The

"seven key points for policy makers" from *Thinking Collaboratively* will help you as you become more involved. Both booklets are available (at $3 each) from the Consortium at 1001 Connecticut Avenue, N.W., Suite 310, Washington, D.C. 20036-5541; or telephone (202) 822-8405.

■ Another useful publication is *Building a Community Agenda: Developing Local Governing Entities*. It is available from the Center for the Study of Social Policy, 1250 Eye Street NW, Suite 503, Washington, D.C. 20005; telephone (202) 371-1565.

■ With support from the U.S. Department of Health and Human Services, the National Center for Service Integration was established in 1991. The Center's purpose is to actively support service integration efforts across the country through an Information Clearinghouse and a Technical Assistance Network.

The Information Clearinghouse, which will be operational by mid-1992, will collect and disseminate information about service integration and maintain a directory of ongoing initiatives. It will be operated by the National Center for Children in Poverty, Columbia University, 154 Haven Avenue, New York, NY 10032, (212) 927-8793. Contact: Terry Bond.

The Technical Assistance Network will attempt to match the needs of local communities with the skills of individuals and organizations with expertise in service integration. For more information, contact Carolyn Marzke at Mathtech, Inc.,

5111 Leesburg Pike, Suite 702, Falls Church, VA 22041 or at (703) 824-7447.

■ Attitudinal barriers are often as formidable as the problems of the various systems that deal with families and children. After all, people have been educated in, and invested their professional lives in, a particular pattern of behavior. The Institute for Educational Leadership (IEL) has created a Collaborative Leadership Development program that can provide technical assistance to your community's leaders as you seek to broaden patterns of thought and behavior. IEL is currently working in Flint, Michigan; Kansas City; Ft. Worth, Texas; and Washington, D.C. In each city, IEL staff is creating a forum that enables the mayor and other political and community leaders to function more effectively across the boundaries that often separate them. IEL also offers a training program focused on the mid-level managers who must make collaboration work. Contact Martin Blank at the Institute for Educational Leadership, 1001 Connecticut Ave. NW, Suite 310, Washington D.C. 20036 or telephone (202) 822-8405. The University of Washington and Florida International University, among others, are also developing interdisciplinary training programs.

■ The Family Resource Coalition is an important resource for communities that are interested in developing neighborhood-based, family-centered prevention and support services. The organization, which has been in existence for ten years, has recently been designated by the U.S. Department of Health and Human Services to serve as the National Resource Center for Family Support Services. It represents more than 2,000 programs and professionals from across the nation and provides information, technical assistance, and training for people involved in family resource and support programs. These programs are not really examples of service integration — they are generally small programs that provide the "glue" or support and empowerment to help families navigate the non-integrated systems. As such, they can be powerful motivators for change, and are presented here as a possible first step to support families, while you are laying the groundwork for larger change and collaboration. Perhaps, with the right leadership, a family resource and support center could become the catalyst your community needs to make collaboration possible. Contact Judy Carter, the Executive Director, at Family Resource Coalition, 200 S. Michigan Avenue, Suite 1520, Chicago, Illinois 60604 or (312) 341-0900.

Notes

1 Huntley-Cooper, Frances. Personal communication, November 1991.
2. Kirst, Michael. Quoted in "Failure By Fragmentation," by Sid Gardner.
3. Gardner, Sid. "Failure By Fragmentation," in *California Tomorrow*, Fall 1989, p. 19.
4. Kusserow, Richard. *Services Integration: A Twenty-Year Retrospective*, Office of Inspector General, Department of Health and Human Services, Washington, D.C. 1991, p. i.
5. New Futures for Little Rock Youth. "Public-Private Partnership Survey," Little Rock, Arkansas, 1989.
6. Dalton, Tom. Personal interview, September 1991.

7. Chatham-Savannah Youth Futures Authority. "We Care About Kids," Savannah, Georgia, 1990, p. 1.

8. Ibid p.2.

9. Ibid.

10. Chatham-Savannah Youth Futures Authority. *Youth Futures Quarterly,* Vol.IV, Issue 1, July 1991.

11. Johnson, Otis. Personal communication, October 1991.

12. Rice, Norman. "Education for the 21st Century: New Challenges, New Opportunities," speech to Strengthening America Commission, June, 1991.

13. Hodge, Woody. Telephone interview, September 1991.

CHAPTER FIVE

Seven Steps to Becoming a More Powerful Partner

1. **Create a focal point for children and family issues.**

2. **Know your own community, its resources, and its needs.**

3. **Establish a children's agenda — know what you want to accomplish.**

4. **Know the players and the systems.**

5. **Network with advocacy groups and with other communities.**

6. **Push a children's agenda on all fronts — government, business, community organizations, and professional associations.**

7. **Ask questions, take risks, and remember the kids!**

Whether you have decided to take the leap into full collaborative planning and service delivery, or you are planning to take incremental bite-size steps toward improving services, there are several things you can do to enhance your performance and your ability to achieve success.

Step 1: Create a Visible Local Focal Point for Children and Family Issues

Every community needs a children's commission or some other public entity whose responsibility it is to focus attention on the issues facing children and families.

There are many models for this public entity. Here are a few, selected from cities across the United States:

■ The Pasadena, California, City Council formed a Commission on Children and Youth made up of local advocates, parents, and professionals to help formulate policy and advise the council. The Commission created the Pasadena Youth Council — an advisory panel of local youth.

■ Mayor Karen Vialle reports that Tacoma, Washington, joined with Pierce County to form the Commission on Children, Youth and Their Families, to generate and coordinate children's policy and to recommend funding priorities to both councils.

■ The Cambridge, Massachusetts, Kids' Council includes representatives of the schools, state agencies, non-profit providers, universities, and the business community, and is charged with coordinating existing programs while increasing access to services and prevention.

■ In Owensboro, Kentucky, Mayor David Adkisson created a Commission on Children In Need, composed mainly of social services agencies, to establish the framework for cooperation and integration.

■ Minneapolis' Youth Coordinating Board is made up of public sector leaders from city, county, and state government entities.

Whether it is local or intergovernmental; made up of lay citizens, youth, or professionals; or is public sector, private sector, or both, your commission must have staff and some degree of independence in order to be effective. As plans and policies are developed, it is important to have a point person within city hall whose responsibility it is to monitor their implementation. This doesn't need to be a new position, but a clear definition of responsibility.

Whatever vehicle you choose, the two most important things to create are **a public setting** in which issues surrounding the well-being of children and their families are top priority and **a mechanism for follow-through** on plans or recommendations. Officials must be clear that this is not just a symbolic gesture, but the beginning of a commitment to engage the major issues facing children and their families.

The remaining six steps will be easier if you have a strong body of committed individuals working with you. But it will still take leadership from you — the elected representative of the people. The need for strong local leadership was clear in virtually every model we reviewed.

Step 2: Know Your Community, its Resources, its Needs

The first, and most important, task you have as you seek to improve services to the families and children in your community is to understand your city's own programs and policies and how they interact both intergovernmentally and with other service providers in your area. You also need to be clear about the needs of your population and the resources available locally to help to meet those needs. The strength of your voice in the intergovernmental arena will be greatly enhanced by your ability to speak knowledgeably about your community.

There are several techniques that have proven to be effective ways for local officials to understand local programs, policies, and problems.

Children's Budget

A separate children's budget shows the kinds and amounts of local resources spent on services to children and families. When this is done by focusing on service areas (child care, protective services, health) rather than organizational units, it can be especially helpful. This kind of service-based (rather than bureaucratically based) budget will also provide a new lens through which to view budget requests. It can help department heads and elected officials begin to ask "How do we increase total community resources for this service?" rather than "How do I increase this departmental budget?"

City budget offices have done a human services budget analysis in Northborough, Massachusetts, and a children's budget in San Francisco. In Bridgeport, Connecticut, a children's budget was prepared by a local advocacy group.

Resource Inventory

Another tool is an inventory of all programs and services for children and families provided by the city, other governmental entities, and private, not-for-profit or for-profit agencies in your community. From this you can gain a sense both for where the gaps and overlaps in service are and how well connected the service providers are.

Dayton, Ohio, did a community-wide inventory of programs and funds and found that much more money was being spent on children's services in their community than they had suspected. The inventory became the basis for Dayton's plan to better utilize existing resources for youth.[1]

Regulatory Review

A review of all city regulatory, licensing, planning, and development functions will iden-tify the direct and indirect impact on children and families of city policies and programs, and it can identify those that may be intergovernmental obstacles. For example, the police department's protocol for handling domestic violence often serves as the city's child abuse policy, and it may or may not be promoting the kind of system you want to have.

One of our survey respondents recommends a "review of city ordinances, zoning, conditional use processes, plan check, permit, business license and other systems to assure that they are as 'user friendly' as possible, and do not impede the development of family housing or support services."[2]

"General plans, zoning, transportation, fire, building and safety, redevelopment, personnel — all these functions must address child and family issues, if a city wants people of childbearing and child rearing years to live or work there. A team approach, involving representatives of all key departments, including the City Attorney, can be very effective."[3]

Property Review

A cross-department review of city-owned land and facilities may help in meeting the needs of children and families. The city of Los Angeles did an "inventory of government property to identify unused or underutilized sites which may be made available at affordable terms for the development of affordable family housing, child care, or related services."[4] It was done with the aid of two graduate students in urban planning from UCLA. When local Head Start providers were looking for new sites to expand services, the city was able to offer surplus city property. Florence Thompson, council member in Bloomsburg, Pennsylvania, reports that by identifying vacant, town-owned land and using FHA financing, the town was able to save a child care center and double its size and capacity.

Analysis of Demographics and Service Needs

Any fiscal and/or policy review of city programs needs to be analyzed in light of a clear understanding of the needs of your population.

As the details from the 1990 census become available, study them carefully for changes in your city's population mix. You cannot plan or advocate successfully for today's families if your notion of who they are is stuck in the 1970s. Are there more single-parent families? Are there more or fewer multi-generational households? Is there a different ethnic, cultural, or racial mix? Is your middle class growing, or are you experiencing a widening of the income gap (increases at the top and bottom)? The answers to all of these questions will guide you as you seek to match the mix of services available in your community to the population.

There are several methods of assessing service needs. Some are more time-consuming or expensive than others. Some focus on building community consensus, while others rely on statistics from ongoing programs, or on the judgment of professionals in the field. Some United Way agencies and universities do regular community needs assessments for their local areas. Even if their area is larger than your community, you may be able to work with them to get the data you need. Ask them to include questions to which you need answers, and ask them to provide you with the responses for only your area.

Where to Get More Information

More information on how to accomplish these review tasks in available in NLC's *Your City's Kids* and *Ways & Means*. The better you understand your city's programs and resources, the clearer you will be about what you need from other governmental entities and what you have to offer.

Step 3: Establish a Children's Agenda: Know What You Want to Accomplish

Becoming an effective advocate on the intergovernmental scene requires that you have clear goals. You must be able to articulate what you wish to accomplish, whether you are working quietly to address a particular problem such as increasing the accessibility of prenatal care or whether you are bringing together whole systems to begin collaborative planning and service delivery such as creation of neighborhood service centers that support and nurture families.

A clear statment of your mission, goals, and priorities can help to galvanize a community into action — especially if its development is broadly based. In dealing with potential funders and other governmental entities, both city government and the nonprofit service providers will benefit from being a part of a city that knows where it wants to go and how it wants to get there.

Some communities have established broad children and family policy frameworks within which they have developed multi-faceted long range plans, set goals and priorities, and established methods for measuring progress. The city of Pasadena, California, has committed itself to being a "Family Community" and has developed seventeen specific implementation strategies. Other cities have chosen to focus their energies on specific areas of need. Rochester, New York, for example, is involved in an Early Childhood Education Initiative.

A major component of knowing what you want to accomplish is determining how your community will know if it is making progress toward its goals. It is not enough to say that you have created ninety or nine hundred new child care spaces, or "served" a hundred more people at the homeless shelter, or had fifteen collaboration meetings. You want to improve the life outcomes for children in your community in some tangible way.

One way to determine the impact of your actions and hold yourselves accountable is to look at the conditions of children today, as measured by reliable indicators, and try to improve those conditions over time. A "scorecard" of several indicators of child and family well-being can be used to track the effectiveness of your activities. Have they succeeded in reducing the number of school dropouts or unmarried teen pregnancies or the infant mortality rate? Both the *KIDS COUNT Data Book* and NLC's *Your City's Kids* offer models of how to collect and use data that can be used to measure outcomes. The national KIDS COUNT effort, funded by the Annie E. Casey Foundation, also supports state-wide efforts with the goal of having KIDS COUNT data collection projects in each state by 1994. The state projects are required to develop county data for the counties in each state. If you want specific information about what is happening in your state, contact Judy Weitz, Director of KIDS COUNT, at the Center for the Study of Social Policy, 1250 Eye Street NW, Suite 503, Washington, D.C. 20005 or at (202) 371-1565.

The important thing here is that you can use your scorecard or data collection process as a tool to help set priorities and actually improve the lives of children and families in some measurable way.

Step 4: Know the Players and the Systems

You already know that it is important to the functioning of your city that you have good relationships with the other elected officials who represent your area at other levels. Many cities have an annual meeting with their members of Congress or state legislators, and perhaps more frequent meetings with county commissioners and school boards. If your city council is not now routinely creating opportunities for such joint sessions, it could be your first suggestion. Given all the homework you have done about the children, resources, and needs in your city, you will have no trouble finding agenda topics.

The tone of these meetings is important. Local leaders want and need intergovernmental partnerships to find shared solutions to shared problems. Bill Barnes of the National League of Cities has observed that the most effective local leaders are those who refuse to be treated like "clients" of the system, simply because they are at the most local or "bottom" of the intergovernmental pyramid. He suggests that effective local leaders insist on being treated as partners and never see themselves as supplicants, merely asking for intergovernmental aid.

Children themselves can often be their own best advocates, if given the chance. Instead of hosting a meeting, take a state legislator, member of Congress, or county commissioner on a tour of a local group home or child care facility in order to personalize your city's kids and your intergovernmental priorities. Decide where to go based on the issues that are important to your city, so that the tour is well thought out, well staffed, and not simply a free photo opportunity. It is also helpful to look for opportunities where children and youths can speak for themselves.

This same kind of "personalization tour" can also be very effective with appointed officials and staff. If you are proud of the way you have made child care available to public housing residents, invite the regional HUD and HHS officials to visit and get some good publicity as well as some good discussion about your municipality's goals.

It can be just as important to know the executive branch agency staff people who actually implement policy decisions as it is to know the chief policy makers themselves. If you are interested in family-based prevention services, you might invite the state or county child welfare services director to address the city council or children's commission on family preservation initiatives.

Another useful strategy for keeping elected or appointed officials up-to-date on what is going on in your municipality is to arrange for them to be invited to speak or respond on a panel at major meetings or conferences held in the area. Knowing what you want to accomplish will help you to target whom to invite. If you need legislative action, you will want your local legislator; if you need a federal waiver, you will try the regional administrator for the program — or that person's boss. Once they agree to speak, you can have city staff offer to provide information on those issues of importance to your city. Their staff will appreciate the help in preparation, and the principal will become fully briefed on what you want him or her to know.

One of the interesting phenomena of intergovernmental relations was revealed in the results of a survey done by Dell Wright and reported in his book, *Understanding Intergovernmental Relations*. People who are elected or are working at each level of government believe that they alone have the broadest perspective. This and other preconceived no-

tions complicate the development of trusting relationships, which are essential to good intergovernmental relations. The wise official will, while seeking good cooperation with counterparts in other government entities, work to understand their point of view, the mandates and stresses they are under, and the fact that they are probably trying to do the best they can with what they've got.

Step 5: Network with Advocacy Groups and Other Communities

One of the best parts of becoming involved in intergovernmental advocacy is that you are suddenly never alone. There is somebody else out there working on just about any issue or problem you are concerned with. In fact, someone has probably written a report or done a study or survey of how your issue is being handled in various states or communities around the country. Appendix A lists state child advocacy groups, and Appendix B lists some of the major national advocacy and professional organizations.

Many cities find that it is an excellent investment to have their department heads keep current with their national and state professional organizations. These organizations notify their members of new studies and publications and when advocacy is needed either at the state or federal level on specific legislative issues. They also monitor federal and state administrative agencies and proposed regulations.

A strong local advocacy voice for children, even if it is not tied directly to city hall, is something to be encouraged, and may produce surprising results. The Bridgeport (Connecticut) Child Advocacy Coalition (BCAC), a private non-profit advocacy group made up, in part, of local service providers, was instrumental in helping the city avoid closing summer recreation and nutrition sites during the summer of 1991. A cooperative relationship between city hall and the Coalition, and the creative redeployment of public and private resources, helped the city through a difficult budget crunch without canceling these important programs.

There are active nonprofit children's advocacy groups in other cities and towns as well, such as San Francisco, Philadelphia, and Greenville, South Carolina.

Allies in child advocacy come in all ages. In order to dispel fears of competition for scarce resources between older Americans and children, several national organizations have banded together in intergenerational collaboration to form "Generations United: A National Coalition on Intergenerational Issues and Programs." Among its notable members are the Child Welfare League of America, American Association of Retired Persons (AARP), Children's Defense Fund, and the National Council on Aging. Any or all of these organizations may be active in your city and could become part of your advocacy network. AARP, nationally, will be placing great emphasis on improving conditions for children, and a local chapter may be able to help in your efforts. *Strategies For Change* is a manual designed to help interested parties build state and local coalitions on intergenerational issues and programs. It is available from Generations United, c/o Child Welfare League of America, 440 First St., NW, Suite 310, Washington, D.C. 20001-2085.

Your community may already have local chapters of some of the national or state advocacy groups. Local advocates and service providers may have a local network of which you and city hall can become a part. On the other hand, it may seem that your community is lacking in advocacy expertise. Nancy Amidei, one of the country's leading child advocates has recently published an advocacy primer: *So You Want To Make A Difference, A Key To Advocacy*. It can be obtained from OMB Watch, 1731 Connecticut Ave. NW, Washington, D.C. 20009-1146; (202) 234-8494. It costs $10 per copy plus shipping.

This wonderful book will unite newcomers and veterans, and just may energize the citizenry to new levels of advocacy — which will very likely include you and the city council. A community united in its advocacy around a common vision is a powerful intergovernmental force.

Step 6: Push a Children's Agenda On All Fronts

Never underestimate the power of an elected official (especially one who has cultivated community advocates) to help set the community agenda. How many speeches do you give in a year? How many receptions do you attend at which you make small-talk and shake hands? How many business and community meetings do you attend? How many boards of directors or advisory boards do you sit on? How often do you attend state-wide or national conferences? How active are you in your state municipal league? All of these are places where your commitment to improving conditions for children and families can have an impact. Use each of them to educate your audience and to enlist them in the advocacy effort. The more specific you can be about what you want to accomplish, and how you are working toward it, the better.

Each organization you belong to, or speak to, or know someone who belongs to, sets an agenda for its activities that should include children and families. If your community has developed a policy framework or long term goals, it makes your job easier, because you will have some specific actions to recommend. But if you haven't, suggest that the organization itself create a study group to determine its most productive contributions.

If you want to know more about what other municipalities are doing, ask the National League of Cities or your state municipal league to schedule workshops specifically on service integration issues or developing a community scorecard on children or intergovernmental advocacy or local collaborative planning.

Step 7: Ask Questions, Take Risks, Remember the Children!

Ask questions at every level — of federal elected and appointed officials, of state legislators and executive branch staff, of county officials, and of your own city planners, program, and budget staff. Don't be afraid to ask things that seem out the ordinary; part of your purpose is to make people think in new ways. This guidebook has suggested various kinds of questions, all of which are important.

Programmatic:

■ Is there a broader way to define the problem and thus the programmatic solution?

■ Is there a way to prevent this problem from occuring?

■ Are services family-centered or structured for the convenience of the providers?

■ How will we measure the success of this program in improving conditions for children and families?

Policy:

■ Are we working within a policy framework that helps us set priorities or are we creating discreet programs to meet the "squeaky wheel" or crisis needs only?

■ What should the balance between prevention, early intervention, and treatment?

■ What can be the role of local government in helping create and test flexibility and innovation in state plans?

Collaboration:

■ How many of us are providing similar services to the same families?

■ Can we consolidate and redirect some of those resources?

■ How are services for similar populations connected?

■ Can we provide "glue" services to keep people from falling through the cracks?

Fiscal:

■ Are we taking full advantage of all available federal and state financial participation?

■ Are we making the best possible use of all existing resources?

■ Can interagency agreements increase access to new resources?

■ What local resources can be used as leverage to draw on resources from other levels?

Always remember why you are involved in this intergovernmental arena in the first place. We are facing the dual crises of the 1990s: Our next generation is growing up in greater poverty and with less hope for the future than any in this century; and our governmental systems cannot respond rationally without radical change.

You, and the leadership you provide both locally and intergovernmentally, can make government work for your city's kids.

Notes:

1. Gardner, Sid. "Failure By Fragmentation," *California Tomorrow*, Fall 1989, p. 25.

2. Lane, Patricia. Response to NLC questionnaire, September 1991.
3. Ibid.

APPENDIX A

State Advocacy Organizations

ALASKA

Action for Alaska's Children
2362 Captain Cook Drive
Anchorage, AK 99517
Phone: 902-248-0834

ARIZONA

Children's Action Alliance
4001 North 3rd Street, #160
Phoenix, AZ 85012
Phone: 602-266-0707

CALIFORNIA

Children Now
660 Thirteenth Street, #300
Oakland, CA 94612
Phone: 415-763-2444

Children Now
1930 14th Street
Santa Monica, CA 90404
Phone: 213-399-7399

COLORADO

Colorado Children's Campaign
1600 Sherman Street, B-300
Denver, CO 80203
Phone: 303-839-1580

FLORIDA

Florida Center for Children and Youth
P.O. Box 6646
Tallahassee, FL 32314
Phone: 904-222-7140

Florida KIDS COUNT Project
Florida Mental Health Institute
University of South Florida
13301 Bruce B. Downs Blvd.
Tampa, FL 33612
Phone: 813-974-4533

GEORGIA

Georgians for Children
530 East Paces Ferry Road, N.E.
Atlanta, GA 30305
Phone: 404-365-8948

HAWAII

Hawaii Advocates for Children and Youth
1154 Fort Street Mall, #305
Honolulu, HI 96813
Phone:

ILLINOIS

Voices for Illinois Children
53 West Jackson, #515
Chicago, IL 60604
Phone: 312-427-4080

INDIANA

Indiana Advocates for Children, Inc.
9135 N. Meridian Street, Suite A-9
Indianapolis, IN 46260
Phone: 317-844-7769

IOWA

Child and Family Policy Center
100 Court Street, Suite 312
Des Moines, IA 50309
Phone: 515-243-2000

KANSAS

Kansas Action for Children
715 S.W. 10th Street
P.O. Box 463
Topeka, KS 66601-0463
Phone: 913-232-0550

KENTUCKY

Kentucky Youth Advocates, Inc.
2034 Frankfort Avenue
Louisville, KY 40206
Phone: 502-895-8167

LOUISIANA

Agenda For Children
P.O. Box 51837
New Orleans, LA 70151
Phone: 504-586-8509

MAINE

Coalition for Maine's Children
P.O. Box 5138
Augusta, ME 04330
Phone: 207-778-3501, ext. 454

MARYLAND

Advocates for Children and Youth
300 Cathedral Street, #140
Baltimore, MD 21201
Phone: 410-547-9200

MASSACHUSETTS

Massachusetts Advocacy Center
95 Berkeley Street, #302
Boston, MA 02116
Phone: 617-357-8431

MICHIGAN

Michigan KIDS COUNT Project
Institute for Children, Youth and Families
2 Paolucci Building
Michigan State University
East Lansing, MI 48824
Phone: 517-336-2660

Michigan KIDS COUNT Project
Michigan League for Human Services
300 N. Washington Square, Suite 401
Lansing, MI 48933
Phone: 517-487-5436

MINNESOTA

Children's Defense Fund–Minnesota
550 Rice Street, Suite 104
St. Paul, MN 55103
Phone: 612-227-6121

MISSISSIPPI

Human Development Center of Mississippi
P.O. Box 68051
Jackson, MS 39286
Phone: 601-355-7784

Mississippi KIDS COUNT Project
Mississippi Office of Policy Development
Division of Budget and Policy
Department of Finance and Administration
455 North Lamar Street
Jackson, MS 39202
Phone: 601-359-6755

MISSOURI

Citizens for Missouri's Children
2717 Sutton Avenue, #200
St. Louis, MO 63143
Phone: 314-647-2003

NEBRASKA

Voices for Children in Nebraska
5005 South 181 Plaza
Omaha, NE 68135
Phone: 402-896-4536

NEVADA

Nevada Alliance for Children
P.O. Box 1503
Crystal Bay, NV 89402
Phone: 702-831-8978

NEW JERSEY

New Jersey KIDS COUNT Project
New Jersey Governor's Committee on
Children's Services Planning
CN 001
Trenton, NJ 08625
Phone: 609-777-1243

Association for Children of New Jersey
35 Halsey Street
Newark, NJ 07102
Phone: 201-643-3876

NEW MEXICO

Coalition for Children
P.O. Box 26666
Albuquerque, NM 87125-6666
Phone: 505-841-1710

NEW YORK

Statewide Youth Advocacy, Inc.
410 Alexander Street
Rochester, NY 14607
Phone: 716-473-0720

NORTH CAROLINA

North Carolina Child Advocacy Institute
1318 Dale Street, Suite 110
Raleigh, NC 27605-1275
Phone: 919-834-6623

NORTH DAKOTA

North Dakota Children's Caucus
311 North Washington
Bismarck, ND 58501
701-255-7229

OHIO

Institute for Child Advocacy
3615 Superior Avenue
Building 31, Fourth Floor
Cleveland, OH 44114
Phone: 216-431-6070

Children's Defense Fund–Ohio
52 E. Lynn Street, Suite 400
Columbus, OH 43215-3507
Phone: 614-221-2244

OKLAHOMA

Oklahoma Institute for Child Advocacy
4030 North Lincoln, #208
Oklahoma City, OK 73105
Phone: 405-424-8014

OREGON

Youth Resources
One SW Columbia, #1720
Portland, OR 97258
Phone: 503-275-9675

PENNSYLVANIA

Pennsylvania Partnerships for Children
3812 Walnut Street
Philadelphia, PA 19104
Phone: 215-387-2707

RHODE ISLAND

Dawn for Children
P.O. Box 3267-09
Providence, RI 02909
Phone: 401-351-2241

SOUTH CAROLINA

Wings for Children
P.O. Box 1962
Myrtle Beach, SC 29578
Phone: 803-448-9294

South Carolina KIDS COUNT Project
South Carolina Budget and Control Board
P.O. Box 12444
609 Wade Hampton Office Building
Columbia, SC 29211
Phone: 803-734-2291

TENNESSEE

Tennessee Commission on Children and Youth
404 James Robertson Parkway, #1510
Nashville, TN 37243-0800
Phone: 615-741-2633

TEXAS

Children's Defense Fund–Texas
316 W. 12th Street, Suite 211
Austin, TX 78701
Phone: 512-472-2223

UTAH

Utah Children
401 12th Avenue, #112
Salt Lake City, UT 84103
Phone: 801-321-5772

WASHINGTON

The Children's Alliance
172 20th Avenue
Seattle, WA 98122
Phone: 206-324-0340

Washington KIDS COUNT Project
Human Services Policy Center
Institute for Public Policy and Management
Graduate School of Public Affairs
University of Washington
324 Parrington, Mail Stop DC-14
Seattle, WA 98195
Phone: 206-543-0190

WEST VIRGINIA

West Virginia Youth Coalition
1205 Quarrier Street, LL
Charleston, WV 25301
Phone: 304-344-3970

West Virginia Task Force on Children, Youth and Families
Suite 406, Atlas Building
1031 Quarrier Street
Charleston, WV 25301
Phone: 304-345-2101

WISCONSIN

Wisconsin Alliance for Children
P.O. Box 1284
Milwaukee, WI 53201-1284
Phone: 414-964-7088

APPENDIX B

National Advocacy, Research, and Professional Organizations

Advisory Commission on Intergovernmental Relations
800 K Street N.W., Suite 450
Washington, D.C. 20575
Phone: 202-653-5540
Fax: 202-653-5429
Contact: Joan Casey, Information Officer

American Association of School Administrators
1801 Moore Street
Arlington, VA 22209
Phone: 703-528-0700
Fax: 703-841-1543
Contact: Bruce Hunter

American Public Welfare Association
810 First Street N.E., Suite 500
Washington, D.C. 20002
Phone: 202-682-0100
Fax: 202-289-6555
Contact: Beverly Yanich, Associate
Director

Association of Child Advocates
Victor Village Place, Suite 101
10 E. Main Street
Victor, NY 14564
Phone: 716-924-0300
Fax: 716-924-4988
Contact: Eve Brooks, President

Center for the Study of Social Policy
1250 Eye Street N.W., Suite 503
Washington, D.C. 20005
Phone: 202-371-1566
Fax: 202-371-1472
Contacts: Tom Joe, Director; Frank
Farrow, Family Preservation

Center on Budget and Policy Priorities
777 N. Capitol St. N.E., Suite 705
Washington, D.C. 20002
Phone: 202-408-1080
Fax: 202-408-1056
Contact: Robert Greenstein, Director

Chapin Hall Center for Children
University of Chicago
1155 East 60th Street
Chicago, IL 60637
Phone: 312-753-5900
Fax: 312-753-5940
Contact: Harold Richman

Child Welfare League of America
440 First Street N.W., Suite 310
Washington, D.C. 20001-2085
Phone: 202-638-2952
Fax: 202-638-4004
Contacts: Shirley Marcus, Deputy Director; Mark Riley, Children's Campaign; Mary Bourdette, Public Policy

Children's Defense Fund
122 C Street N.W., Suite 400
Washington, D.C. 20001
Phone: 202-628-8787
Fax: 202-783-7324

Council of Chief State School Officers
400 N. Capitol Street, N.W.
Washington, D.C. 20001
Phone: 202-393-8159
Fax: 202-393-1228

Council of Governors' Policy Advisors
400 N. Capitol Street, N.W.
Washington, D.C. 20001
Phone: 202-624-5386
Fax: 202-624-7846

Education Commission of the States
707 17th Street
Suite 2700
Denver, CO 80202-3427
Phone:303-299-3600

Elementary School Center
2 E. 103rd Street
New York, NY 10029
Phone: 212-289-5929
Fax: 212-289-6019

Family and Work Institute
330 Seventh Avenue, 14th Floor
New York, NY 10001
Phone: 212-465-2044
Fax: 212-465-8637
Contacts: Ellen Galinsky, Co-president; Dana Friedman, Co-president

Family Resource Coalition
200 South Michigan Avenue, Suite 1520
Chicago, IL 60604
Phone: 312-341-0900
Fax: 312-341-9361
Contact: Judy Langford Carter, Executive Director

Generations United
c/o Child Welfare League of America
440 First Street N.W.
Washington, D.C. 20001-2085
Phone: 202-638-2952
Fax: 202-638-4004
Contact: Tess Scannell

House Select Committee on Children, Youth and Families
H2-385 Ford House Office Building
Washington, D.C. 20515
Phone: 202-226-7660
Fax 202-226-7672
Contact: Karabelle Pizzigati, Executive Director

Institute for Educational Leadership
1001 Connecticut Avenue N.W., Suite 310
Washington, D.C. 20036
Phone: 202-822-8405
Fax: 202-872-4050
Contact: Martin Blank, Senior Associate

International City County Management Association
777 N. Capitol Street, N.E., Suite 500
Washington, D.C. 20002-4201
Phone: 202-962-3673
Fax: 202-962-3500
Contact: Mary Grover

Kids Count
1250 Eye Street N.W., Suite 503
Washington, D.C. 20005
Phone: 202-371-1566
Fax: 202-371-1472
Contact: Judith Weitz, Coordinator

Kiwanis International
3636 Woodview Trace
Indianapolis, IN 46268-3196
Phone: 317-875-8755; 800-879-4769
Fax: 317-879-0204

**National Alliance of Business
Center for Excellence in Education**
1201 New York Avenue N.W., Suite 700
Washington, D.C. 20005
Phone: 202-289-2888
Fax: 202-289-1303
Contact: Terri Bergman, Director of
Program Activities

**National Assembly of National Voluntary
Health and Social Welfare Organizations**
1319 F Street N.W., Suite 601
Washington, D.C. 20004
Phone: 202-347-2080
Fax: 202-393-4517
Contact: Gordon Raley, Executive
Director

**National Association for the
Education of Young Children**
1834 Connecticut Avenue N.W.
Washington, D.C. 20009
Phone: 202-232-8777
Fax: 202-328-1846
Contact: Barbara Willer, Public Affairs
Director

National Association of Counties
440 First Street, N.W., 8th Floor
Washington, D.C. 20001
Phone: 202-393-6226
Fax: 202-393-2630
Contacts: Don Murray; Tom Joseph

**National Association of
State Boards of Education**

1012 Cameron Street
Alexandria, VA 22314
Phone: 703-684-4000
Fax: 703-836-2313

**National Association of
Towns and Townships**
1522 K Street, N.W.
Washington, D.C. 20005
Phone: 202-737-5200
Fax: 202-289-7996
Contact: Jeffrey Schiff

**National Black Child Development
Institute**
1023 15th Street N.W., Suite 600
Washington, D.C. 20005
Phone: 202-387-1281
Fax: 202-234-1738
Contact: Evelyn Moore, Executive
Director

National Conference of State Legislatures
1560 Broadway, Suite 700
Denver, CO 80202-5140
Phone: 303-830-2200
Fax: 303-863-8003

National Governors' Association
444 North Capitol N.W., Suite 250
Washington, D.C. 20001
Phone: 202-624-5300
Fax: 202-624-5321

National School Boards Association
1680 Duke Street
Alexandria, VA 22314
Phone: 703-838-6760
Fax: 703-683-7590
Contacts: Martharose Laffey; Dorothy
Clarke

U. S. Conference of Mayors
1620 Eye Street, N.W.
Washington, D.C. 20006
Phone: 202-293-7330
Fax: 202-293-2352
Contact: Laura Waxman

APPENDIX C

References and Further Reading

American Association of School Administrators. *Beyond the Schools, How Schools & Communities Must Collaborate to Solve the Problems Facing America's Youth,* Arlington, VA 1991.

American Public Welfare Association and National Association of Housing and Redevelopment Officials. *Family Self-Sufficiency: Linking Housing, Public Welfare and Social Services,* Washington, D.C. 1990.

Amidei, Nancy. *So You Want to Make A Difference: A Key to Advocacy,* OMB Watch, Washington, D.C. 1991.

Anton, Thomas. *Intergovernmental Relations in the U.S.: The Next Wave of Change,* National League of Cities, Washington, D.C. 1988.

Bell, Dan. *What States Can Do to Secure a Skilled and Stable Child Care Work Force: Strategies to Use the New Federal Funds for Child Care Quality,* Child Care Employees Project, Oakland, CA 1991.

Blank, Helen. *The Child Care and Development Block Grant and Child Care Grants to States Under Title IV-A of the Social Security Act: A Description of Major Provisions and Issues to Consider in Implementation,* Children's Defense Fund, Washington, D.C. 1991.

Blank, Martin J. and Lombardi, Joan. *Towards Improved Services for Children and Families: Forging New Relationships through Collaboration,* Institute for Educational Leadership, Washington, D.C. 1992.

Blank, Martin J. and Melaville, Atelia I. *What it Takes: Structuring Interagency Partnerships to Connect Children and Families with Comprehensive Services,* Education and Human Services Consortium, Washington, D.C. 1991.

Breyel, Janine and Hill, Ian T. *Caring for Kids: Strategies for Improving State Child Health Programs,* National Governors' Association, Washington, D.C. 1991.

Bruner, Charles. "Is Change from Above Possible? State-Level Strategies for Supporting Street-Level Services," *The Early Adolescence Magazine,* Vol.V, No.4, March-April 1991, pp.29-39.

Bruner, Charles. *Thinking Collaboratively: Ten Questions and Answers to Help Policy Makers Improve Children's Services,* Education and Human Services Consortium, Washington, D.C. 1991.

The Annie E. Casey Foundation and Center for the Study of Social Policy. *KIDS COUNT Data Book: State Profiles of Child Well-Being,* Washington, D.C. 1992.

Center for the Study of Social Policy. *Building a Community Agenda: Developing Local Governing Entities,* Washington, D.C. 1991.

Center for the Study of Social Policy. *Leveraging Dollars, Leveraging Change: Refinancing and Restructuring Children's Services in Five Sites,* Washington, D.C. 1991.

Center on Budget and Policy Priorities. *The States and the Poor,* Washington, D.C. 1991.

Children's Defense Fund. *Children 1990: A Report Card, Briefing Book, and Action Primer,* Washington, D.C. 1990.

Children's Defense Fund. *An Opinion Maker's Guide to Children in Election Year 1992,* Washington, D.C. 1992.

Children's Defense Fund. *The State of America's Children 1991,* Washington, D.C. 1991.

Chynoweth, Judith K. and Dyer, Barbara R. *Strengthening Families: A Guide for State Policymaking,* Council of Governors' Policy Advisors, Washington, D.C. 1991.

Committee for Economic Development. *An America That Works: The Life-Cycle Approach to a Competitive Work Force,* New York, NY 1990.

Gold, Steven D. *Reforming State-Local Relations: A Practical Guide,* National Conference of State Legislatures, Denver, CO 1989.

Heller Graduate School, Center for Human Resources. *Managing Community Planning and Action Projects: A Series of Cases to Assist Senior Project Staff Think Through the Always Messy Process of Implementation,* Brandeis University, Waltham, MA 1991.

Hodgkinson, Harold L. *The Same Client: The Demographics of Education and Service Delivery Systems,* Institute for Educational Leadership, Washington, D.C. 1989.

Jeffery, Blake; Salant, Tanis; and Boroshok, Alan. *County Government Structure: A State by State Report,* National Association of Counties, Washington, D.C. 1989.

Kusserow, Richard P. *Services Integration: A Twenty-Year Retrospective,* U.S. Department of Health and Human Services, Office of Inspector General, Washington, D.C. 1991.

McKnight, John and Kretzman, John. *Mapping Community Capacity,* Northwestern University, Center for Urban Affairs and Policy Research, Evanston, IL.

National Coalition for an Urban Children's Agenda. *Implementing the Children's Agenda: Critical Elements of System-Wide Reform,* Alexandria, VA 1991.

National Commission on Children. *Beyond Rhetoric: A New American Agenda for Children and Families,* Washington, D.C. 1991.

National Task Force on School Readiness. *Caring Communities: Supporting Young Children and Families,* National Association of State Boards of Education, Alexandria, VA 1991.

Ooms, Theodora and Priester, Stephen, editors. *A Strategy for Strengthening Families: Implementing Family Criteria in Policymaking and Program Evaluation,* The Family Impact Seminar, Washington, D.C. 1988.

Potapchuk, William and Bailey, Margaret. *Building Collaborative Communities: A Selective Bibliography for Community Leaders,* Program for Community Problem Solving, Washington, D.C. 1991.

Richman, Harold; Wynn, Joan; and Costello, Joan. *Children's Services in Metropolitan Chicago: Directions for the Future,* University of Chicago, Chapin Hall Center for Children, Chicago, IL 1991.

Robison, Susan D. *Putting the Pieces Together: Survey of State Systems for*

Children in Crisis, National Conference of State Legislatures, Denver, CO 1990.

Select Committee on Children, Youth, and Families, U.S. House of Representatives. *Opportunities for Success: Cost-Effective Programs for Children, Update 1990,* Washington, D.C. 1990.

Shanahan, Eileen. "Going it Jointly: Regional Solutions for Local Problems," in *Governing,* August, 1991.

Ventura-Merkel, Catherine. *Strategies for Change: Building State and Local Coalitions on Intergenerational Issues and Programs,* Generations United, Washington, D.C. 1990.

Wright, Dell S. *Understanding Intergovernmental Relations,* Washington, D.C. 1988.

ABOUT THE
AUTHOR

Bonnie Armstrong, an independent consultant on child and family policy issues and intergovernmental relations, has more than twenty years experience in human services at all levels of government and in the private sector. She lives in Pasadena, California, where she has chaired the city's Commission on Children and Youth and guided the development of a City Policy for Children, Youth and Families. During the 1970s, as an aide to Florida Governor Reubin Askew, she was instrumental in the statewide integration and decentralization of Florida's state human services systems. She also worked in Washington, D.C. as an advocate for more flexible, rational, and client-centered programs. She currently serves as a board member or advisor for many state, county, and local organizations and is a vocal advocate for children and families. As the mother of two pre-teenagers, she feels deeply the need to improve conditions for all children.

NOTES

NOTES

NOTES

NOTES

NOTES

NOTES

NOTES

NOTES

Publications Available Through The Project

Our Future and Our Only Hope: A Survey of City Halls Regarding Children and Families. Highlights results of a 390 city survey concerning problems and needs of children and families in cities, including 250 brief success stories. For children, lack of child care, substance abuse, and education were the top rated problems needing attention. For families, a shortage of affordable housing, especially low-income housing, topped the list of needs. ISBN 0-933729-52-9; NLC Order #8003; $15 each

Your City's Kids. Booklet designed to help local officials identify problems and develop solutions to cope with the needs of children in their communities. Discusses information resources available on children and poses questions about existing program coordination and long-term strategy development. It explains why local officials should be interested, what questions they should ask about children in their communities, and where the answers can be found. NLC Order #8009; single copies free

Children, Families & Cities: Programs that Work at the Local Level. Provides analyses of issues and three dozen project profiles of local efforts to deal with child care, youth employment, teen pregnancy prevention, child and family homelessness, and strategic planning. Includes "lessons learned," project contacts, and discussion of local strategic planning and integrated program delivery. ISBN 0-933729-32-4; NLC Order #8008; $15 each

Local Officials Guide to Family Day Care Zoning. Provides practical guidance on how cities can create and operate needed home-based child care facilities within the context of local zoning regulations. Discusses planning and siting issues, problems and solutions to local zoning rules that may limit or prohibit the provision of family day care in residential neighborhoods, licensing, traffic, parking, noise, and density considerations, and model solutions. Ap-

pendix lists child care resource and referral agencies. ISBN 0-933729-54-5; NLC Order #8002; $20 each

Caring for Children: Case Studies of Local Government Child Care Initiatives. Describes the increasing involvement of municipalities in child care issues. This case study report highlights examples of successful local government child care programs from 24 cities across the country. Details varying local roles in child care involvement, including provision of space and utilities, subsidies, benefits for city employees, zoning, after school programs, training, and resource and referral. Highlights lessons learned. ISBN 0-933729-53-7; NLC Order #8001; $20 each

Ways and Means for Children and Families. Provides information on funding sources for city programs to assist children and families. Examines the role of local government as a broker or provider of services; highlights the availability and use of federal, state, and private funding sources; discusses ways to organize and administer local programs; and provides examples of model programs and lists of resources. ISBN 0-933729-61-8; NLC Order #8004; $35 each

Making Government Work for Your City's Kids: Getting Through the Intergovernmental Maze of Programs for Children and Families. Designed to help local elected officials act as effective advocates for children and families by asking the right questions, holding other levels and units of government accountable, and making local concerns heard. Describes how to deal with the intergovernmental maze of programs, services, plans, and policies which come from county, state, and federal governments. Clarifies the roles of various levels of government and identifies key decision points where local input can be especially effective. ISBN 0-933729-71-5; NLC Order #8010; $30 each

Prices shown are current as of May 1992. All prices are subject to change.

- -

Publications Department, National League of Cities
1301 Pennsylvania Avenue NW, Washington, D.C. 20004
Please send me the following publications:

Title	NLC Order #	No. of Copies	Price
_____	_____	_____	_____
_____	_____	_____	_____
_____	_____	_____	_____
_____	_____	_____	_____
_____			

Postage and Handling: $ 4.00
Amount Enclosed: _____

Name: _____
Address: _____
_____
City, State, ZIP: _____

NOTES